Mastering Depreciation

by
Garo Kalfayan, J.D., LLM., C.P.A.
Professor, Department of Accountancy
The Sid Craig School of Business
California State University
Fresno, California

Denise M. Patterson, Ph.D., C.P.A.
Professor, Department of Accountancy
The Sid Craig School of Business
California State University
Fresno, California

Garo Kalfayan, J.D., LL.M., CPA., is Professor, Department of Accountancy, The Sid Craig School of Business, California State University, Fresno, California

Denise M. Patterson, Ph.D., CPA, is Professor, Department of Accountancy, The Sid Craig School of Business, California State University, Fresno, California.

Design: Moss Design, Bethesda, MD
Typesetting: Lovelady Consulting, Roswell, GA

© AIPB, 1999, 2000, 2003, 2004, 2007
ISBN 1-884826-28-8

This publication is designed to provide accurate and authoritative information in regard to the subject matter covered. It is sold with the understanding that the publisher and author are not engaged in rendering legal, accounting or other professional services. If legal advice or other expert assistance is required, the services of a competent professional person should be sought.—From a Declaration of Principles jointly adopted by a Committee of the American Bar Association and a Committee of Publishers and Associations.

INTRODUCTION

Mastering Depreciation covers everything you need to know for the depreciation portion of the *Certified Bookkeeper* examination. If you take the optional open-book Final Examination at the end of this workbook, achieve a grade of at least 70, then become a *Certified Bookkeeper,* you can receive retroactively 7 Continuing Professional Education Credits (CPECs).

Anyone who achieves a grade of at least 70 on the optional Final Examination, receives an AIPB *Certificate of Completion.*

When you have completed this course, you should be able to:

1. Understand how qualifying assets are depreciated on the financial statements and tax return.

2. Depreciate for book purposes assets purchased at any time during the year under the straight-line, units of production, declining balance, and sum-of-the-years'-digits methods.

3. Depreciate both listed assets and real-estate for tax purposes.

4. Depreciate vehicles, including passenger automobiles, for tax purposes.

***Important*:** This course is current as of the date of publication, June 1, 2007. Because tax laws are always changing, double-check the latest corporate tax rates, depreciation rates, and other rates when you are completing your company's or client's tax returns. Also, check for changes in the tax law, new IRS pronouncements, and recent court cases that may affect the return.

A note on rounding errors: To make this course as easy as possible to learn, depreciation rates are generally rounded. For example, a depreciation rate of 33.3333% will be rounded to 33%. When that 33% (rather than 33.3333%) depreciation rate is multiplied by $200,000, it results in a rounding error of $660. When the rounded rate is applied year after year, the error may become significant. For teaching purposes, however, rounding errors seemed preferable to endless decimal places.

To get the most out of the course, we suggest the following:

1. Read the concise narrative that begins each section.

2. Read the narrative again. This time, cover the solution and try to figure out each problem. *Actually write it out.* By *trying* to solve the problem and checking your answer against the correct solution, you will learn a great deal.

3. Take Quiz #1 at the end of each section to see what you learned and what you need to review.

4. Take Quiz #2 at the end of each section to master any points you missed.

Lastly, please take a moment to fill out and send in the Course Evaluation at the back (whether or not you take the final). It will help us to improve this and other courses.

Enjoy the course—and congratulations on taking a major step toward advancing your professional knowledge and career.

CONTENTS

INTRODUCTION iii

Section 1
**DEPRECIATION ON THE FINANCIAL STATEMENTS
V. TAX RETURN** 1

Section 2
DEPRECIATION UNDER GAAP (FOR BOOK PURPOSES) 13

Section 3
THE STRAIGHT-LINE METHOD OF DEPRECIATION 31

Section 4
**THE UNITS OF PRODUCTION METHOD
OF DEPRECIATION** 59

Section 5
**THE DECLINING BALANCE METHOD
OF DEPRECIATION** 89

Section 6
**THE SUM-OF-THE YEARS'-DIGITS METHOD
OF DEPRECIATION** 117

Section 7
**DEPRECIATION UNDER FEDERAL INCOME TAX
DEPRECIATION RULES** 145

Section 8
**TAX DEPRECIATION OF PASSENGER CARS
AND OTHER VEHICLES** 179

FINAL EXAMINATION (Optional) 199

FINAL EXAMINATION ANSWER SHEET 213

COURSE EVALUATION 215

Section 1
DEPRECIATION ON THE FINANCIAL STATEMENTS V. TAX RETURN

Introduction

Depreciation is a system of allocating (spreading out) the cost of plant and equipment assets, often referred to as fixed assets, over their estimated life. Land is not depreciated. The purpose of spreading out an asset's cost over several years is to match this cost with the revenue that the asset helps the company earn each year. The amount of cost allocated each year is *depreciation expense*, or simply *depreciation*. Depreciation is recorded at the end of each year—generally, a calendar year, but for some companies a fiscal* year. Depreciation may be recorded more frequently, such as at the end of each month or quarter. The following adjusting journal entry is used to record depreciation.

       Depreciation Expense
          Accumulated Depreciation

For example, if your company owned a machine and computed this year's depreciation expense at $2,000, the adjusting entry on December 31 would be as follows:

Depreciation Expense	2,000	
Accumulated Depreciation		2,000

Depreciation Expense is an income statement account. When the income statement is prepared, the balance in this account will be presented with other expenses as depreciation expense. Manufacturers will present a portion of depreciation for those assets used to manufacture their products with manufacturing costs as part of cost of goods sold (this is explained later in the course). Accumulated Depreciation is a balance sheet account. The balance in this account shows total depreciation expense taken in all years to date.

---

* A fiscal year is any 12-month period that a company chooses as its accounting period.

Computing Depreciation
for Book v. Tax Purposes

There are two sets of depreciation rules: the Internal Revenue Service (IRS) rules, which must be used to compute depreciation for the tax return; and rules under Generally Accepted Accounting Principles (GAAP), which must be used to compute depreciation for the financial statements. GAAP depreciation rules are required for the financial statements because they more closely match an asset's cost with the revenue that the asset helps earn over its life. Many small companies that do not need audited financial statements use tax depreciation methods for both their tax return and their financial statements.

Why There Are Two Ways
to Compute Depreciation Expense

A company that prepares financial statements for a third party, such as a bank (to obtain a loan) for potential investors, or for a company that may want to acquire it, must use GAAP rules rather than IRS rules to compute depreciation. All publicly traded companies must use GAAP for their financial statements, which are filed with the Securities and Exchange Commission (SEC) and other government agencies.

Companies that use GAAP must compute depreciation twice: once under GAAP for their financial statements; once under IRS rules for their federal tax return. The computation for the tax return is not recorded on the books.

EXAMPLE 1: In 20X7, FuCo computes annual depreciation using GAAP rules at $40,000 and computes depreciation using tax rules at $50,000. The adjusting journal entry recorded in the general ledger on December 31, 20X7, uses only the GAAP amount as follows:

Depreciation Expense	40,000	
Accumulated Depreciation		40,000

The $50,000 depreciation expense deducted on the tax return is not recorded in the general ledger.

Procedures for Computing Depreciation Under GAAP

Generally, a company that is preparing financial statements under GAAP for a third party must have a CPA who is independent (unrelated to the company) go over the statements to assure that the statements are properly prepared. The CPA will perform one of three services:

1. A *compilation*. The independent CPA organizes the company's financial data into the various financial statements, usually following industry format, but does not express an opinion on the reliability (accuracy) of the statements or whether they conform to GAAP. In fact, CPAs often put together financial statements for the company using whatever facts and figures the company has provided, including tax depreciation, and add a note stating that the statements are based only on the information provided by the company.

2. A *review*. The independent CPA provides a report describing his or her limited inspection of the financial statements and stating that he or she did not find any material difference from GAAP rules.

3. An *audit*. The independent CPA examines the company's financial statements and expresses an opinion on whether they materially conform to GAAP rules.

A CPA's preparation of a company's income tax return is not considered involvement with the financial statements and, like a compilation, does not require the CPA to use GAAP depreciation rules.

Materiality

A CPA doing a review or audit does not have to make sure that depreciation expense on the company's financial statements is the exact amount calculated under one of the GAAP depreciation methods. As long as the difference between depreciation on the statements and the GAAP calculation is not *material*, the difference can be ignored. This allows many companies to use tax depreciation on their financial statements. Because tax depreciation rules are based on many of the same concepts as GAAP depreciation rules, the difference between the two calculations is often not material. Thus, if a company can use tax depreciation for both tax and book purposes, it can avoid having to record one amount in the general ledger and another amount on the tax return.

EXAMPLE 2: In 20X5, BaCo calculates tax depreciation at $50,000 and book depreciation under GAAP at $52,000. If the CPA determines that the $2,000 difference is not material, depreciation will be presented on the reviewed or audited statements at $50,000.

Summary

The purpose of depreciation expense is to match an asset's cost with the revenues that it helps the company earn in each period. This must be computed as follows:

- Companies that do not have to present financial statements that have been reviewed or audited by a CPA can use tax depreciation for both their tax return and their financial statements.

- Companies that must present financial statements that have been reviewed or audited by a CPA must use GAAP rules to compute depreciation expense for their financial statements and must use tax rules for the tax return.

A CPA who does a review or audit of a company's financial statements must use GAAP depreciation, but may use tax depreciation for the statements if the difference between the tax and GAAP amounts is not material.

QUIZ 1 **DEPRECIATION ON THE FINANCIAL STATEMENTS V. TAX RETURN**

Problem I.

Mark each statement True or False.

1. Whether a company uses GAAP rules or tax rules to compute depreciation recorded in the financial statements depends upon how the company uses its financial statements.

    a. True   b. False

2. If a company's year-end financial statements are to be reviewed by a CPA, the depreciation amount for the statements is generally computed under GAAP rules.

    a. True   b. False

3. Even if a company's tax and GAAP depreciation expense are not materially different, a CPA conducting an audit will require the company to use the amount computed under GAAP.

    a. True   b. False

Problem II.

Multiple choice. Circle the correct answer.

1. The adjusting entry to record $5,000 of depreciation expense in the general ledger is . . .

a. Depreciation Expense	5,000	
Accumulated Depreciation		5,000
b. Depreciation Expense	5,000	
Depreciation Payable		5,000
c. Depreciation Payable	5,000	
Depreciation Expense		5,000
d. Accumulated Depreciation	5,000	
Depreciation Expense		5000

2. Which of the following does *not* require using an independent CPA?

    a. An audit of company financial statements
    b. Preparation of the company tax return
    c. A review of the company's financial statements
    d. An opinion on whether the financial statements materially conform to GAAP rules

3. If a company is required to have an audit of its financial statements, then . . .

    a. GAAP depreciation must be the same as tax depreciation.
    b. If GAAP depreciation is materially different from tax depreciation, the company must use the GAAP amount for its financial statements and the tax amount for its tax return.
    c. GAAP depreciation must always be used for the company's financial statements even if tax depreciation is not materially different.
    d. It does not matter whether the company uses GAAP or tax depreciation.

Problem III.

Fill in the blanks.

1. The balance sheet account showing total depreciation expense taken to date is _____ _____.

2. Depreciation _____ the cost of an asset over its estimated life.

3. The purpose of depreciation is to _____ the asset's cost to the revenue that it helps the organization earn each year over its life.

QUIZ 1   Solutions and Explanations

Problem I.

1. True

If a company does not need its financial statements reviewed or audited by a CPA, it can use the tax depreciation amount on its financial statements.

2. True

If the financial statements are to be reviewed by a CPA, either depreciation must be computed under GAAP rules or the tax depreciation amount cannot differ materially from the GAAP depreciation amount.

3. False

If the difference between GAAP and tax depreciation is not material, the tax amount can be used for book purposes (that is, for the financial statements).

Problem II.

1. a

Depreciation Expense is an income statement expense account and is increased with a debit. Accumulated Depreciation is a balance sheet account and is increased with a credit. There is no Depreciation Payable account because there is no liability or cash paid.

2. b

An audit, review or opinion about whether the financial statements materially conform to GAAP rules requires an independent CPA. The tax return may be prepared by anyone the company chooses. Although many companies use a CPA to prepare the company's tax return, this is not required.

3. b

Depreciation computed under GAAP rules is used for financial statements unless the amount computed under IRS tax rules is not materially different from the GAAP amount.

Problem III.

1. Accumulated Depreciation

2. allocates (spends)

3. match

QUIZ 2   **DEPRECIATION ON THE FINANCIAL STATEMENTS V. TAX RETURN**

Problem I.

Mark each statement True or False.

1. Annual depreciation expense is the amount of cash a company sets aside to replace a plant or equipment asset.

    a. True   b. False

2. Depreciation expense computed under tax or GAAP rules is not materially different.

    a. True   b. False

3. A company that wants a CPA to do a review of its financial statements depreciates its plant and equipment assets under GAAP for its federal income tax return.

    a. True   b. False

4. Many of the concepts underlying tax depreciation rules are similar to the concepts underlying GAAP depreciation rules.

    a. True   b. False

Problem II.

Multiple choice. Circle the correct answer.

1. A company is required to have an independent CPA audit its year-end financial statements if . . .

    a. the company needs to file an income tax return.
    b. the company must demonstrate that its financial statements conform with GAAP.
    c. the company's stock is publicly traded.
    d. b and c.

2. Which of the following statements is true?

    a. If depreciation expense under GAAP is not very different from depreciation under federal income tax rules, the GAAP amount can be used on the federal income tax return.

    b. If depreciation expense under federal income tax rules is not materially different from depreciation expense under GAAP, the company can use the tax amount on its financial statements and a CPA reviewing the statements may not have to change this amount.

    c. Both a and b are true.

3. The most detailed work on a company's financial statements is performed in . . .

    a. an audit.

    b. a review.

    c. a compilation.

Problem III.

Fill in the blanks.

1. Financial statements prepared for company management (do/do not) _____ have to use GAAP depreciation rules.

2. If a company uses the tax depreciation amount on its financial statements, a CPA performing an audit will require the company to adjust depreciation expense if the difference between the tax amount and the GAAP amount is _____.

3. If a company prepares its financial statements under GAAP, it (does/does not) _____ have to use a CPA to prepare company income tax returns.

QUIZ 2   Solutions and Explanations

Problem I.

1. False
Depreciation expense does not involve cash. It is the portion of an asset's cost "used up" (taken as an expense) during the period.

2. False
Although depreciation expense computed under tax and GAAP rules *may be* almost the same, it is just as likely to be very different.

3. False
A company that wants a CPA to do a review of its financial statements must depreciate its plant and equipment assets under GAAP only for its financial statements. Depreciation on the tax return must always use tax rules.

4. True

Problem II.

1. d

2. b

3. a

Problem III.

1. do not

2. material

3. does not

Section 2

DEPRECIATION UNDER GAAP (FOR BOOK PURPOSES)

Introduction

Most plant and equipment assets wear out or become obsolete over the years. Similarly, although land is not depreciated (because it does not wear out), improvements to land, such as paving or fences, are depreciated because these improvements wear out or become obsolete over time. As described in Section 1, the portion of the asset "used up" (worn out) each year is depreciation expense, or simply depreciation. Depreciation for each asset is usually calculated separately and is based on four factors:

a. the asset's cost;
b. the asset's estimated life;
c. the asset's residual value (its book value after being fully depreciated); and
d. the method of depreciation selected.

Determining the Asset's Cost

For depreciation purposes, the cost (*historical cost, original cost* or *acquisition cost*) is more than just the invoice price. It includes *any cost incurred to acquire, transport and prepare the asset for its intended use,* such as sales tax, commissions, title fees, transportation, and installation.

EXAMPLE 1: CuCo purchases a machine that has the following breakdown of costs: Invoice price, $20,000, sales tax, $1,500, freight, $500, outside contractor to install the machine, $200. For depreciation purposes, the cost of the machine is $22,200, computed as follows:

$20,000	invoice price
1,500	sales tax
500	freight
200	set-up (contractor)
$22,200	total cost

Thus, CuCo records acquisition of the machine as follows:

Asset—Machine	22,200	
Cash		22,200

Group Purchases

Sometimes a company pays a single price for a group of assets and cannot tell from the invoice how much of the freight, installation and other costs are attributable to each asset. Moreover, because one asset may have a life of three years, another five years and so on, and because other assets in the group may not even be depreciable (such as the land in an acquisition of five adjacent buildings), the company allocates a separate cost for each asset.

The price of each asset in a group purchase is computed as follows:

$$\frac{\text{Specific asset's fair market value (FMV)}}{\text{Total FMV of all assets acquired}} = rate \; x \; total \; acquisition \; cost = specific \; asset's \; acquisition \; cost$$

PROBLEM 1: MiCo's purchase of a computer, printer and a copier has an acquisition cost of $6,000. The invoice does not separately list the cost of each item. What is the acquisition cost of each asset?

SOLUTION 1: MiCo estimates, or obtains from a formal appraisal, the FMV of each asset, as follows:

Asset	FMV
Computer	$4,000
Printer	1,000
Copier	3,000
Total FMV	$8,000

Next, MiCo computes each asset's portion of the total $6,000 acquisition cost, as follows:

1. To compute the acquisition cost of the computer:

$$\frac{\$4,000 \text{ computer FMV}}{\$8,000 \text{ total FMV}} = 0.5 \; rate \; x \; \$6,000 \; total \; acquisition \; cost = \$3,000 \; acquisition \; cost \; for \; the \; computer$$

2. To compute the acquisition cost of the printer:

$$\frac{\$1,000 \text{ printer FMV}}{\$8,000 \text{ total FMV}} = 0.125 \; rate \; x \; \$6,000 \; total \; acquisition \; cost = \$750 \; acquisition \; cost \; for \; the \; printer$$

3. To compute the acquisition cost of the copier:

$$\frac{\$3,000 \text{ copier FMV}}{\$8,000 \text{ total FMV}} = 0.375 \; x \; \$6,000 \; total \; acquisition \; cost = \$2,250 \; acquisition \; cost \; for \; the \; copier$$

To summarize the acquisition cost of each asset, individually:

Asset	Acquisition cost
Computer	$3,000
Printer	750
Copier	2,250
Total cost	$6,000

PROBLEM 2: SaCo's purchase of a building and land has a total original cost (acquisition cost) of $100,000. The purchase contract does not separately list the price of the building and the land. The company estimates the following FMVs for the building and land:

Asset	FMV
Building	$ 75,000
Land	50,000
Total FMV	$125,000

What is the acquisition cost of the building for depreciation and recordkeeping purposes? What is the original cost of the land (for recordkeeping purposes only, because land cannot be depreciated)?

SOLUTION 2: SaCo allocates the original cost of the building and land as follows:

1. To compute allocation of the original cost of the building:

$$\frac{\$75,000 \text{ building FMV}}{\$125,000 \text{ total FMV}} = 0.6 \text{ x } \$100,000 \text{ total original cost} = \$60,000 \text{ original cost of building}$$

2. To compute allocation of the original cost of the land:

$$\frac{\$50,000 \text{ building FMV}}{\$125,000 \text{ total FMV}} = 0.4 \text{ x } \$100,000 \text{ total original cost} = \$40,000 \text{ original cost of land}$$

Contributed Assets

It is common practice in startup and even in established companies for owners to contribute assets rather than cash in exchange for stock. The computations and journal entries for contributed assets under GAAP or tax rules are done by a CPA and are not included in this course.

Determining the Asset's Estimated Life

The estimated life is the number of years the company expects the asset to last or the amount of production it expects from the machine measured in hours, miles, units produced, or any other standard. For example, a machine's life may be measured in years of expected use or units of expected production; an automobile in years or miles or hours of expected use; a building in years of expected use.

Determining the Asset's Residual Value (or Scrap Value or Salvage Value)

The residual value is an estimate made by company management of the dollar amount that can be recovered for the asset at the end of its useful life when it is disposed of (sold or traded in). This amount cannot be depreciated. When the residual value is subtracted from the acquisition cost, the remainder is the full amount that can be depreciated and is referred to as the *depreciable base*.

Acquisition cost − residual value = depreciable base

To put it another way, when total depreciation taken on an asset equals the depreciable base, the asset has been fully depreciated.

For example, if XyCo buys a $20,000 packaging machine and estimates that at the end of the machine's useful life it will have a residual value of $1,000, the machine's depreciable base is $19,000. XyCo can take a total of $19,000 in depreciation expense over the machine's useful life. If, instead, XyCo estimates that the machine will have no residual value at the end of its life, then the original cost of $20,000 is the depreciable base, and XyCo can take $20,000 in depreciation expense over the machine's useful life.

Selecting a Depreciation Method

Under GAAP, a plant or equipment asset can be depreciated using one of four basic methods:

1. The straight-line (SL) method. The asset is depreciated by dividing the depreciable base (acquisition cost − residual value) by the number of years in the estimated life to determine each year's depreciation expense. Thus, under SL, each year's depreciation expense is the same.

2. The units of production (UOP) or units of output method.
The asset is depreciated each year according to the number of units produced, total hours used, total miles driven, or other measure of production. Thus, under UOP, the amount of annual depreciation fluctuates by output or use.

3. The accelerated methods. There are two methods of accelerated depreciation. They are called accelerated because they provide more annual depreciation expense in the earlier years of the asset's life and less depreciation expense in the later years. The two accelerated methods are the *declining balance* (DB) method and the *sum-of-the-years'-digits* (SYD) *method*, which are explained in this course in Sections 5 and 6 respectively.

Regardless of the depreciation method selected or annual depreciation taken, total depreciation over the life of the asset is the same.

How Depreciation Is Recorded

When depreciation expense is recorded at the end of the year, quarter, month or other period, the same accounts are debited or credited in the adjusting journal entry regardless of the method used; only the amount of depreciation will be different. Depreciation expense is generally recorded just before a company prepares its financial statements. Although some companies prepare statements quarterly, and therefore record depreciation expense quarterly, most firms prepare their statements annually. As noted in Section 1, the journal entry used to record depreciation is:

Depreciation Expense
    Accumulated Depreciation

Often, there is only one Depreciation Expense account, but a separate Accumulated Depreciation account for each group of assets that a firm presents on its balance sheet, such as Accumulated Depreciation—Equipment and Accumulated Depreciation—Vehicles. This is the method used in this course. (Some firms may have an accumulated depreciation account for each asset, such as Accumulated Depreciation—Boiler or Accumulated Depreciation—Crane, then group the accumulated depreciation accounts at the end of the period for the balance sheet.)

The depreciation expense account is an income statement account and, reflects the total cost of plant assets expensed (allocated) against revenue for the *current* period.

The accumulated depreciation account is a balance sheet account. It increases each time depreciation is recorded. It represents a running total of all depreciation taken to date for plant assets which remain on hand (have not been disposed of) including *prior and current* periods.

The typical balance sheet shows property and equipment separately under the heading "Plant, property and equipment," so the typical company will have at least two accumulated depreciation accounts: Accumulated Depreciation—Buildings, and Accumulated Depreciation—Equipment (equipment is plant). Many firms also have accumulated depreciation accounts for subcategories of assets, such as vehicles (Accumulated Depreciation—Vehicles). The accounts might appear in the general ledger as follows:

> Asset—Office Building
> Asset—Garage
> Asset—Warehouse
> Accumulated Depreciation—Buildings
> Asset—Truck
> Asset—Auto
> Asset—Forklift
> Accumulated Depreciation—Vehicles
> Asset—Computer
> Asset—Drillpress
> Accumulated Depreciation—Equipment

PROBLEM 3: On January 3, 20X5, HaCo purchases a computer for $10,000 cash, then takes $1,000 depreciation in 20X5, the year of purchase, and $1,000 in 20X6. In which accounts does HaCo record the acquisition? The 20X5 depreciation expense? The 20X6 depreciation expense?

SOLUTION 3: HaCo records the acquisition as follows:

<u>January 3, 20X5</u>

Asset—Computer	10,000	
Cash		10,000

HaCo records the 20X5 depreciation expense as follows:

<u>December 31, 20X5</u>

Depreciation Expense	1,000	
Accumulated Depreciation—Computer		1,000

HaCo records the 20X6 depreciation expense as follows:

December 31, 20X6
Depreciation Expense   1,000
    Accumulated Depreciation—Equipment   1,000
To record depreciation expense

Note that after recording the 20X6 depreciation expense, the balance in Accumulated Depreciation—Equipment is $2,000 ($1,000 depreciation for 20X5 + $1,000 depreciation for 20X6).

Computing Book Value

Book value, or net book value, does not represent an asset's fair market value. Instead, it represents the undepreciated cost of the asset as it appears on the company's books and balance sheet. Book value is the acquisition cost less accumulated depreciation (accumulated depreciation is all depreciation expense taken on the asset to date). To put it in a simple formula:

Acquisition cost − accumulated depreciation = book value

For instance, for HaCo in the example above, the book value of its computer at the end of 20X6 is $8,000. To compute:

$10,000 acquisition cost − $2,000 accumulated depreciation = $8,000 book value

How Manufacturing Companies Record Depreciation

Manufacturing companies record depreciation in two ways:

1. Depreciation for machines, buildings, or other fixed assets used in the manufacture of products is recorded in the Inventory account (*not* in Depreciation Expense) as follows:

Inventory—Work-In-Process OH*
    Accumulated Depreciation—[Buildings, Equipment, etc.]
*overhead

Note: In actual practice, manufacturers record depreciation for the period in the Manufacturing Overhead account. As items are produced, depreciation related to the manufactured items is transferred from Manufacturing Overhead to Inventory—Work-In-Process. However, because a detailed understanding of depreciation for manufacturers is not required for this course, we record depreciation related to manufacturing in the account Inventory—Work-In-Process OH (overhead). As work in process is completed and sold, a proportional amount of the depreciation expense will be transferred to Finished Goods Inventory and then to Cost Of Goods Sold.

2. Depreciation for machines, buildings, or other fixed assets used by a manufacturing company for nonmanufacturing activities, such as office furniture, is recorded in Depreciation Expense, as follows:

Depreciation Expense
    Accumulated Depreciation—[Buildings, Equipment, etc.]

When assets are used for both manufacturing and nonmanufacturing purposes, such as a building that holds both administrative and production facilities or an air-conditioning system that cools both production and office space, depreciation is allocated proportionally between Inventory and Depreciation Expense as follows:

Inventory—Work-In-Process OH
Depreciation Expense
    Accumulated Depreciation—[Buildings, Equipment, etc.]

When work in process is eventually completed and sold, the depreciation will be transferred to Finished Goods Inventory and then to Cost Of Goods Sold.

PROBLEM 4: For 20X5, SyCo Manufacturing allocates $10,000 of depreciation as follows: $2,000 for manufacturing machinery and $8,000 for a building. Syco determines that 75% of the building is used for manufacturing. What adjusting entries does SyCo record at year end to recognize depreciation?

SOLUTION 4: First, Syco must compute how much of the $8,000 depreciation for the building to allocate to manufacturing v. office use. To compute: $8,000 building depreciation x 75% manufacturing use = $6,000 of depreciation allocated to manufacturing. The remaining $2,000 is recorded in Depreciation Expense ($8,000 building depreciation x 25% office use = $2,000).

Therefore, SyCo records the year-end adjusting entries for depreciation as follows:

Depreciation Expense   2,000*
    Accumulated Depreciation—Building   2,000

*This is the $2,000 of the building's depreciation allocated to office use.

Inventory—Work-In-Process OH	8,000**	
Accumulated Depreciation—Equipment		2,000
Accumulated Depreciation—Building		6,000

**$6,000 of the building's depreciation allocated to manufacturing + $2,000 depreciation for the manufacturing machinery.

Depreciation on the Financial Statements

Reporting on the income statement. Nonmanufacturing companies report depreciation expense on the income statement under operating expenses as a selling and administrative expense. Manufacturing companies report some depreciation as an operating (selling and administrative) expense and include some in the expense cost of goods sold in the year that the products it manufactures are sold.

Reporting on the balance sheet. Plant and equipment assets appear on the balance sheet in the property, plant and equipment section. For example, buildings might be presented as follows:

Buildings at acquisition cost
– Accumulated depreciation
Book value

As accumulated depreciation increases over the years or other periods, the asset's current book value decreases. An illustration of plant assets on the balance sheet would appear as follows:

Property, plant and equipment (PP&E):		
Land—at cost		75,000
Buildings—at cost	1,000,000	
Less: Accumulated depreciation	100,000	900,000
		975,000

Land—at cost. Land is not depreciated, so this amount does not change from year to year.

Buildings—at cost. This is the acquisition cost of *all* buildings, the total of the balances in all the building accounts (Asset—Building, Asset—Warehouse, etc.). The acquisition cost appears unchanged on the balance sheet year after year until the asset is sold or traded.

Accumulated depreciation. This is the balance in the account Accumulated Depreciation—Buildings.

Although the words "book value" do not appear, the book value, or net book value of the property, plant and equipment is the $975,000 total and the book value of the buildings is $900,000. Thus, having an accumulated depreciation account for each group of assets presented on the balance sheet provides an easy way to compute and show the net book value for that group of assets.

Equipment assets are presented in a similar way:

> Equipment at acquisition cost
> – accumulated depreciation
> current book value   (as of the balance sheet date).

The building and equipment assets appear on the balance sheet as follows:

Property, plant and equipment (PP&E):

Land—at cost		75,000
Buildings—at cost	1,000,000	
Less: Accumulated Depreciation	100,00	900,000
Equipment—at cost	25,000	
Less: Accumulated depreciation	4,400	**20,600**
Total PP&E		995,600

Equipment—at cost. This is the acquisition cost of *all* the equipment, the total of the balances in all the equipment accounts (Asset—Truck; Asset—Computer; Asset—Drillpress; etc.). The acquisition cost appears unchanged on the balance sheet year after year until the asset is sold or traded.

Accumulated depreciation. This is the balance in Accumulated Depreciation—Equipment.

Although the words "book value" do not appear, the book value, or net book value, does appear. The current net book value of all equipment is $20,600, and the current net book value of all property, plant and equipment is $995,600.

Sometimes the balance sheet will show assets at net (that is, the accumulated depreciation was subtracted from the original cost before the amount was presented on the balance sheet):

Property, plant and equipment (PP&E):

Land—at cost	75,000
Buildings—at net	900,000
Equipment—at net	20,600
Total PP&E	995,600

QUIZ 1 — DEPRECIATION UNDER GAAP (FOR BOOK PURPOSES).

Problem I.

Mark each statement True or False.

1. The total amount of depreciation taken over the life of the asset is the same regardless of which depreciation method is selected.

    a. True   b. False

2. Net book value is a year-end estimate of the fair market value of a company's depreciable assets.

    a. True   b. False

3. The balance sheet shows the acquisition cost and the accumulated depreciation of each asset.

    a. True   b. False

Problem II.

Multiple choice. Circle the correct answer.

1. Which of the following assets is *not* depreciable?

    a. building   b. machine   c. fence   d. land

2. Which of the following is an income statement account?

    a. Asset—Machine
    b. Accumulated Depreciation—Equipment
    c. Depreciation Expense
    d. Inventory—Work-In-Process OH

3. Which depreciation method is *not* based on the number of accounting periods in which an asset is used?

    a. straight line
    b. units of production
    c. declining balance
    d. sum-of-the-years'-digits

Use the following information for Questions 4–7: SuCo pays $50,000 cash for a machine, $3,500 cash in sales tax and $1,500 cash for shipping and set up.

4. What is the machine's cost for depreciation purposes?

    a. $10,000   b. $50,000   c. $53,500   d. $55,000

5. What is the journal entry (omitting dollar amounts) to record the purchase of the machine?

    a. Asset—Machine
            Accumulated Depreciation—Equipment
    b. Depreciation Expense
            Accumulated Depreciation—Equipment
    c. Asset—Machine
            Cash
    d. Asset—Equipment
            Depreciation Expense

6. If a nonmanufacturing company can take $5,000 in depreciation for the year, what is the journal entry to record the depreciation?

    a. Asset—Machine   5,000
          Accumulated Depreciation—Equipment   5,000
    b. Depreciation Expense   5,000
          Accumulated Depreciation—Equipment   5,000
    c. Depreciation Expense   5,000
          Asset—Machine   5,000
    d. Accumulated Depreciation—Equipment   5,000
          Depreciation Expense   5,000

7. If a manufacturing company can take $5,000 in depreciation for a machine used totally for the production of inventory, what is the journal entry to record the depreciation?

    a. Inventory—Work-In-Process OH   5,000
           Accumulated Depreciation—Equipment   5,000
    b. Inventory—Work-In-Process OH   5,000
           Asset—Machine   5,000
    c. Depreciation Expense   5,000
           Inventory—Work-In-Process OH   5,000
    d. Inventory—Work-In-Process OH   5,000
           Depreciation Expense   5,000

QUIZ 1   Solutions and Explanations

Problem I.

1. True

Although some methods result in the same amount of depreciation in each year of an asset's life, other methods take more depreciation in the early years, less in the later years. Still other methods result in depreciation varying from year to year depending on usage. Regardless of which method is used, however, *total* depreciation over an asset's life is the same under all methods.

2. False

Book value, or net book value, is shown on the company's books (acquisition cost less accumulated depreciation) and is unrelated to the asset's fair market value.

3. False

The balance sheet shows the *total* acquisition cost and the *total* accumulated depreciation of company assets.

Problem II.

1. d

Land is not depreciable (it is not subject to wear and does not have a limited life).

2. c

Depreciation Expense is an income statement account. Asset—Machine, and Inventory—Work-In-Process OH are assets and therefore balance sheet accounts. Accumulated Depreciation, the contra account to Equipment, is also a balance sheet account.

3. b.

The units of production method is based on an asset's usage and not on the number of periods (years, quarters, etc.) in which the asset is used.

4. d

An asset's acquisition (or original or historical) cost for depreciation purposes includes the invoice price plus all costs related to the purchase plus all costs required to put it into use. To compute: $50,000 invoice price + $3,500 sales tax + $1,500 shipping = $55,000 acquisition cost.

5. c

6. b

7. a

Depreciation of assets used to manufacture inventory is allocated to Inventory—Work-In-Process OH rather than to Depreciation Expense to account for the portion of the machine's cost used to produce the inventory.

QUIZ 2   DEPRECIATION UNDER GAAP (FOR BOOK PURPOSES)

Problem I.

Multiple choice. Circle the correct answer.

Use the following information for Questions 1 and 2: BiCo gets a good deal on a computer and color copier by paying a total invoice price of $30,000 for both. The company estimates the computer's FMV at $24,000 and the copier's FMV at $8,000.

1. BiCo will record the acquisition cost of the computer at . . .

   a. $22,500   b. $24,000   c. $30,000   d. $32,000

2. BiCo will record the acquisition cost of the copier at . . .

   a. $30,000   b. $8,000   c. $7,500   d. $32,000

3. The period over which a business expects to use an asset is called the asset's . . .

   a. estimated life.
   b. residual value.
   c. depreciable base.
   d. recovery period.

4. The undepreciated portion of an asset's cost at the end of an asset's useful life is the asset's . . .

   a. estimated life.
   b. residual value (or salvage value).
   c. depreciable base.
   d. original cost.

5. Which of the following is not a depreciation method?

    a. sum-of-the-year's-digits
    b. declining balance
    c. straight-line
    d. residual value

6. Which of the following is needed to calculate depreciation on an asset under GAAP?

    a. original cost
    b. useful life
    c. depreciation method
    d. salvage value
    e. all of the above

Problem II.

Use the following facts to answer Questions 1 and 2: QuitCo's sole asset is a $50,000 machine that has first-year depreciation of $3,000 and second-year depreciation also of $3,000.

1. Show how the asset and accumulated depreciation will appear on the company's balance sheet at the end of the first year.

2. What is the book value of the company's property, plant and equipment at the end of the first year?

QUIZ 2   Solutions and Explanations

Problem I.

1. a

To compute:

$$\frac{\$24,000 \text{ computer FMV}}{\$32,000 \text{ total FMV}} = 0.75 \text{ x } \$30,000 \text{ total cost} = \$22,500 \text{ acquisition cost for the computer}$$

2. c

To compute:

$$\frac{\$8,000 \text{ copier FMV}}{\$32,000 \text{ total FMV}} = 0.25 \text{ x } \$30,000 \text{ total cost} = \$7,500 \text{ acquisition cost for the copier}$$

3. a

4. b

5. d

6. e.

Problem II.

1. At the end of the first year, the asset and accumulated depreciation
will appear on the company's balance sheet as follows:

Property, Plant, and Equipment (PP&E):
Equipment—at cost	$50,000
Less: Accumulated depreciation	$ 3,000
Total PP&E	$47,000

2. $47,000

At the end of the first year, the balance in Accumulated
Depreciation is only $3,000 because only one year's depreciation
has been taken. To compute: $50,000 original cost – $3,000
accumulated depreciation for 1 year = $47,000 book value (also
referred to as net book value)

THE STRAIGHT-LINE METHOD OF DEPRECIATION

Introduction

A company that expects an asset to provide equal benefits in each year of its estimated life should select the straight-line method of depreciation. Under this method, the same amount of depreciation expense is taken every year and can be computed in one of two ways:

The first way is the easiest. Simply divide the depreciable base by the estimated life:

$$\frac{\text{Depreciable base*}}{\text{Years of estimated life}} = \text{annual depreciation expense}$$

*Original cost – residual value = depreciable base

The second way is to compute an annual *depreciation rate*:

$$\frac{1.00}{\text{Years of estimated life}} = \begin{array}{l}\text{annual depreciation rate (\% of depreciable} \\ \text{base taken for depreciation)}\end{array}$$

Annual depreciation rate x depreciable base = annual depreciation expense

PROBLEM 1: GliCo acquires a fixed asset for $45,000 and estimates a residual value of $5,000 and an estimated life of 5 years. What is the annual depreciation expense under the straight-line method?

SOLUTION 1: First compute the depreciable base: $45,000 acquisition cost – $5,000 residual value = $40,000 depreciable base.

You can now compute annual depreciation expense in two ways:

1. To compute depreciation expense simply using years:

$$\frac{\$40,000 \text{ depreciable base}}{5 \text{ years (estimated life)}} = \$8,000 \text{ annual depreciation expense}$$

2. To compute depreciation expense using an annual depreciation rate:

$$\frac{1.00}{5 \text{ years (estimated life)}} = 20\% \text{ annual depreciation rate}$$

20% annual depreciation rate x $40,000 depreciable base = $8,000 annual depreciation expense

PROBLEM 2: On January 1, FaCo acquires equipment with an invoice cost of $90,000, sales tax of $7,000 and delivery and installation costs of $3,000. Management expects the equipment to last 10 years, at which point it will have a residual value of $10,000. The equipment will be depreciated using the straight-line method.

    1. What is the acquisition cost?
    2. What is the depreciable base?
    3. What is the annual depreciation computed using (a) years?
       (b) a depreciation rate?
    4. What is the year-end adjusting entry to record depreciation?

SOLUTION 2:

1. To compute the acquisition cost (invoice cost plus all costs required to make the asset ready for its intended use):

$ 90,000	invoice cost
7,000	sales tax
3,000	delivery and installation costs
$100,000	acquisition cost

2. To compute the depreciable base:

  $100,000 acquisition cost – $10,000 residual value =
  $90,000 depreciable base

3a. To compute annual depreciation using years:

$$\frac{\$90,000 \text{ depreciable base}}{10 \text{ years (estimated life)}} = \$9,000 \text{ annual depreciation expense}$$

3b. To compute annual depreciation using a depreciation rate:

$$\frac{1.00}{10 \text{ years (estimated life)}} = 10\% \text{ depreciation rate}$$

$90,000 depreciable base x 10% depreciation rate =
$9,000 annual depreciation expense

Because most companies compute straight-line depreciation using years, this will be the approach in this course.

4. To record depreciation expense in the year-end adjusting entry:

Depreciation Expense	9,000	
Accumulated Depreciation—Equipment		9,000

Under the straight-line method, $9,000 of depreciation will be recorded in each of the 10 years of the equipment's estimated life.

Note: Under GAAP, depreciation cannot begin until the asset has been acquired *and* placed in service. However, to avoid cumbersome, repetitious language ("on January 1, FaCo acquires and places in service ...") it is assumed throughout this course that the acquired asset is placed in service on the date of purchase.

Depreciating an Asset Acquired During the Year

For assets acquired *during* the year, such as on June 1, depreciation is recorded for only a portion of the first year. GAAP requires that the method that is used to prorate depreciation in the first year be reasonable and consistently used (that is, used for all fixed assets).

Some companies prorate first-year depreciation by using the actual number of days the asset is in service for the year. Other firms use the number of months. Still other businesses have a policy of depreciating any asset acquired between the 1st and 15th of the month as though it were acquired at the beginning of the month, and of depreciating any asset acquired between the 15th and the end of the month as if it were acquired at the beginning of the following month.

For example, if a company acquires equipment on June 10, it can depreciate it starting on June 1. But if the equipment is acquired on June 23, the company would depreciate it starting on July 1.

PROBLEM 3: On June 1, 20X7 CriCo, which has a calendar year, purchases equipment with an acquisition cost of $70,000, an estimated life of 5 years and a residual value of $10,000. What is first-year depreciation if CriCo prorates first-year usage by the number of months the equipment is used?

SOLUTION 3: First, compute the depreciable base: $70,000 acquisition cost – $10,000 residual value = $60,000 depreciable base.

Next, compute the annual depreciation rate:

$$\frac{\$60,000}{5 \text{ years}} = \$12,000 \text{ annual depreciation expense}$$

To allocate first-year depreciation by number of months:

7/12 x $12,000 = $7,000 first-year depreciation*

$$*\frac{\$12,000 \text{ annual depreciation expense}}{12 \text{ months}} = \$1,000/\text{mo. x 7 mos. (June-Dec.)} = \$7,000 \text{ first-year dep.}$$

Note that because CriCo purchased the equipment in June, it will record for 20X7 depreciation expense of only $7,000 (7 months x $1,000). The remaining $5,000 will be taken in the last year, the sixth calendar year in which the company owns the asset.

Tracking Depreciation Over the Life of the Asset

PROBLEM 4: On January 1, BarCo acquires equipment that costs $100,000. Management estimates that the equipment will have a 10-year life and will have a residual value of $10,000. Thus, the asset's depreciable base is $90,000 ($100,000 original cost – $10,000 residual value). What is the annual depreciation, accumulated depreciation and book value in each year of the asset's life?

SOLUTION 4: First compute annual depreciation: $100,000 acquisition cost – $10,000 residual value = $90,000 depreciable base ÷ 10 years (estimated life) = $9,000 annual depreciation.

The following table shows the annual depreciation, accumulated depreciation and book value in each year of the asset's life:

Year ending	Depreciation expense for the year	Credit to Accum. Depreciation	Year-end balance in Accum. Depreciation	Year-end book value
01/01/X1				$100,000*
12/31/X1	$9,000	$9,000	$ 9,000	91,000
12/31/X2	9,000	9,000	18,000	82,000
12/31/X3	9,000	9,000	27,000	73,000
12/31/X4	9,000	9,000	36,000	64,000
12/31/X5	9,000	9,000	45,000	55,000
12/31/X6	9,000	9,000	54,000	46,000
12/31/X7	9,000	9,000	63,000	37,000
12/31/X8	9,000	9,000	72,000	28,000
12/31/X9	9,000	9,000	81,000	19,000
12/31/X10	9,000	9,000	90,000	10,000

* This is the acquisition cost.

As each year passes, the balance in Accumulated Depreciation increases and the book value (acquisition cost less total accumulated depreciation) decreases. At the end of 20X1, the book value is $91,000 ($100,000 acquisition cost – $9,000 total accumulated depreciation = $91,000 book value). At the end of 20X2, the book value is $82,000 ($100,000 acquisition cost – $18,000 total accumulated depreciation = $82,000 book value) and so on.

In the last year of the asset's 10-year life, the balance in Accumulated Depreciation is equal to the depreciable base of $90,000 because the asset is fully depreciated (no more depreciation can be taken even if the company continues to use the asset). Also in the last year, the asset's book value—the value that will appear on the company's books and balance sheet—is equal to the residual value of $10,000.

PROBLEM 5: Same facts as Problem 4, but this time the purchase is made on June 1. BarCo acquires equipment costing $100,000. Management estimates that the equipment will have a 10-year life and a residual value of $10,000. What is the annual depreciation, accumulated depreciation and book value in each year of the asset's life?

SOLUTION 5: First compute annual depreciation (the computation isthe same regardless of the month in which the asset is acquired): $100,000 acquisition cost – $10,000 residual value = $90,000 depreciable base ÷ 10 years (estimated life) = $9,000 annual depreciation expense. The following table illustrates the annual depreciation, accumulated depreciation and book value in each year of the asset's life:

Year ending	Depreciation expense for the year	Credit to Accum. Depreciation	Year-end balance in Accum. Depreciation	Year-end book value
06/01/X1 (purchase date)				$100,000*
12/31/X1	($9,000 x 7/12) = $5,250	$5,250	$ 5,250	94,750
12/31/X2	9,000	9,000	14,250	85,750
12/31/X3	9,000	9,000	23,250	76,750
12/31/X4	9,000	9,000	32,250	67,750
12/31/X5	9,000	9,000	41,250	58,750
12/31/X6	9,000	9,000	50,250	49,750
12/31/X7	9,000	9,000	59,250	40,750
12/31/X8	9,000	9,000	68,250	31,750
12/31/X9	9,000	9,000	77,250	22,750
12/31/X10	9,000	9,000	86,250	13,750
12/31/X11	($9,000 x 5/12) = $3,750	3,750	90,000	10,000

* This is the acquisition cost.

Note that depreciation for Year 1 plus depreciation for Year 11 equals $9,000, the normal depreciation for 1 year. The reason is that when an asset is acquired during the year, depreciation is allocated between the first and last time periods. Year 1 depreciation of $5,250 is for the 7 months that the asset was used (June 1–December 31). To compute: $9,000 x $\frac{7}{12}$ = $5,250. The remaining $3,750 ($9,000 annual depreciation expense – $5,250 taken in the first year = $3,750 remaining) is taken in Year 11 for the 5 months that the asset was used (January 1–May 31).

Preparing the Depreciation Schedule

Almost all textbooks refer to tables like the ones shown on pages 35 and 36 as depreciation schedules. But most on-the-job accounting professionals use a schedule that presents the current year's depreciation expense and perhaps depreciation from prior years but not depreciation for future years. Almost every accounting firm will have its own little wrinkles on its depreciation schedule, but most contain the date on which the asset was purchased, the depreciation method and the depreciation expense for the current year.

The schedule lists all of the company's depreciable assets, even those that were fully depreciated years ago. It may or may not list assets that are not depreciable, such as land (it may show land with no depreciation taken). When the schedule is completed at the end of the period, a photocopy will be made. The copy will be stapled to the worksheet (on which the unadjusted trial balance is extended to the adjustments, adjusted trial balance and financial statement columns) along with other schedules and references to support the worksheet and become part of the work papers. (Work papers are the worksheet and all supporting documentation including the schedules.)

On the following page is an illustration of an actual depreciation schedule used by a small accounting firm for its clients for the past 25 years. This firm, like most others that use a manual (rather than computerized) depreciation schedule, has designed the schedule with its own special twists. For example, the schedule shown on the next page does not list the units of production method under "Methods" (because this firm never uses this method), has the column heading "depreciable cost" rather than "depreciable base" (either is correct), and has a column for residual value (you will see other schedules that do not). Schedules printed from various computer software packages may also have different formats.

Depreciation Schedule

Methods
SSL = straight line
DB = declining balance
SD = sum-of-the-years'-digits

KIND OF PROPERTY	DATE ACQUIRED	METHOD	RATE OR LIFE	DEPRECIABLE COST OR OTHER BASIS	RESIDUAL (SALVAGE) VALUE	DEPRECIATION IN PRIOR YEARS	DEPRECIATION FOR YR. ENDED	ACCUMULATED DEPRECIATION	DEPRECIATION FOR YR. ENDED	ACCUMULATED DEPRECIATION	DEPRECIATION FOR YR. ENDED	ACCUMULATED DEPRECIATION

Using the Depreciation Schedule

The beginning of this section explained how to compute annual depreciation expense under the straight-line method. On the job, you would compute depreciation for all depreciable assets, write the amounts on the schedule, copy the amounts from the schedule to the worksheet, and later the amount into the general journal as the adjusting entry for depreciation.

Note that the schedule does not show how much depreciation is recorded to the Depreciation Expense account and how much goes to Inventory—Work-In-Process OH (overhead). It shows only total depreciation taken for the year. In a manufacturing company, the allocation of depreciation to Depreciation Expense or Inventory—Work-In-Process OH depends on how much each asset was used for nonmanufacturing v. manufacturing purposes.

Regardless of how many assets appear on the schedule, the adjusting journal entry will debit only the total depreciation for all assets to Depreciation Expense and/or Inventory—Work-In-Process OH and will credit the two or three Accumulated Depreciation Expense accounts as needed.

For example, suppose that PlatCo, a manufacturer of dishware, prepares its financial statements under GAAP and presents at the end of 2006 the depreciation schedule shown on the following page.

Depreciation Schedule (2006)

Methods
SSL = straight line
DB = declining balance
SD = sum-of-the-years'-digits

KIND OF PROPERTY	DATE ACQUIRED	METHOD	RATE OR LIFE	DEPRECIABLE COST OR OTHER BASIS	RESIDUAL (SALVAGE) VALUE	DEPRECIATION IN PRIOR YEARS	DEPRECIATION FOR YR. ENDED 12/31/04	ACCUMULATED DEPRECIATION 12/31/04	DEPRECIATION FOR YR. ENDED 12/31/05	ACCUMULATED DEPRECIATION 12/31/05	DEPRECIATION FOR YR. ENDED 12/31/06	ACCUMULATED DEPRECIATION 12/31/06
Property												
Office Building	1/5/00	SL	30 yrs	300,000	100,000	40,000	10,000	50,000	10,000	60,000	10,000	70,000
Land for ofc. bldg.	1/5/00	NA		55,000								
Warehouse	11/12/72	SL	4%	90,000	25,000	90,000		90,000		90,000		90,000
Land for warehouse	11/12/72	NA		32,000								
Equipment												
Boiler (80% man.)	1/1/01	SL	15 yrs.	75,000	10,000	15,000	5,000	20,000	5,000	25,000	5,000	30,000
Air filter (100% man.)	7/2/03	SL	8 yrs	88,000	5,000	5,500	11,000	16,500	11,000	27,500	11,000	38,500
Vehicles												
Chevrolet Nova *Sold 1/2/06*	1/1/00	SL	5 yrs.	15,000	3,000	12,000	3,000	15,000	-0-	15,000	SOLD	
Oldsmobile	11/3/04	SL	6 yrs.	18,000	6,000		500	500	3,000	3,500	3,000	6,500
Delivery van (used)	1/14/05	SL	20%	20,000	5,000				4,000	4,000	4,000	8,000
Totals				693,000	154,000	162,500	29,500	192,000	33,000	225,000	33,000	243,000

Note the following:

- This schedule is a continuation of previous schedules not shown, but all the information needed is included.

- Land, which was included in the purchase of both the office building and the warehouse, is included on the schedule even though it is not depreciated because most firms show *all* assets on the depreciation schedule.

- The warehouse, fully depreciated years ago, remains on the schedule because PlatCo still owns it. All the assets that a company owns appear on the schedule every year, even after they are fully depreciated.

- At the beginning of 2004, the air filter had only $5,500 accumulated depreciation ("depreciation in prior years") because it was purchased on July 2, 2003, and therefore was depreciated for only 6 months in 2003. To compute:

$$\frac{\$88,000 \text{ depreciable cost}}{8 \text{ years}} = \begin{array}{c} \$11,000 \text{ annual depreciation x } \frac{1}{2} \text{ year (July–December)} = \\ \$5,500 \text{ depreciation in 2003} \end{array}$$

- Included in the description of the boiler is the phrase "80% man." so that anyone who reads the schedule will know that the 80% of the depreciation for the boiler is recorded to Inventory—Work-In-Process OH and the 20% used for the offices is recorded to Depreciation Expense. There are an endless number of ways to do this. For example, the company could note instead the percentage for office use. Or it could have one schedule for assets used in the office, another for assets used for manufacturing. There are still other variations.

- Because the Chevrolet Nova was fully depreciated by year-end 2004, there is no depreciation expense for 2005. However, in 2005, total accumulated depreciation is still on the schedule because the asset had not yet been sold and is therefore still in the books.

- Depreciation for the Oldsmobile in the first year is $500 because in the year of purchase it was depreciated for only 2 months (November and December).

- The accounting department chose to use a percentage rate instead of number of years to depreciate the warehouse and the van. The warehouse apparently has an estimated life of 25 years (1.00/25 = 4%) and the van an estimated life of 5 years (1.00/5 years = 20%).

But how can PlatCo be sure that it has depreciated all of the company's depreciable assets? In other words, how can it make sure that an asset was not omitted from the schedule and therefore not depreciated for 2006?

In doing the depreciation for PlatCo, you would follow these steps:

1. Total the depreciable cost column, then total the residual value column. Sum the totals from the two columns to yield the total acquisition cost of all assets that PlatCo is depreciating in 2006: To compute:

$693,000	total "depreciable cost or other basis" of all assets on the depreciation schedule
+154,000	total residual value of all assets on the depreciation schedule
$847,000	total acquisition cost of all assets on the depreciation schedule

2. Subtract the acquisition cost of any assets on the schedule that were sold during 2006:

$847,000	total acquisition cost of all assets on the depreciation schedule
− 18,000	Chevrolet Nova acquisition cost ($15,000 depreciable cost + $3,000 residual value)
$829,000	total acquisition cost of all assets owned by the company at year-end 2006

To verify the depreciation schedule, go to the general ledger, find all the plant and equipment asset accounts and add all the balances (the balance in each account is the acquisition cost). The total should be $829,000. If the total of all depreciable asset account balances is more than $829,000, then PlatCo has omitted an asset. If the total is less than $829,000, then the schedule may list an asset that the company no longer owns, or there may be an error.

Now it is easy to see why PlatCo included land on the depreciation schedule: it made checking the depreciation schedule against the general ledger asset accounts much easier. If land had been left off the schedule, then the accounting department would have had to add the balances of only the *depreciable* accounts, increasing the likelihood of errors and undermining the crosscheck.

Two adjusting entries are required to record PlatCo's depreciation expense for 2006. The first entry allocates depreciation for nonmanufacturing assets to the Depreciation Expense account. The second entry allocates depreciation for manufacturing assets to Inventory—Work-In-Process OH.

To make the proper allocation, you need the following information: The factory air filter is used 100% for the factory. The boiler is used 80% for the factory and 20% for the office.

Depreciation Expense		18,000*
Accumulated Depreciation—Buildings		10,000
Accumulated Depreciation—Equipment		1,000
Accumulated Depreciation—Vehicles		7,000

*$10,000	office building
1,000	boiler ($5,000 depreciation x 20% office use, as noted on the schedule)
3,000	Oldsmobile
4,000	delivery van
$18,000	

The second entry allocates all the depreciation for the factory air filter and 80% of the boiler to the Inventory—Work-In-Process OH[1] account:

Inventory—Work-In-Process OH		15,000*
Accumulated Depreciation—Equipment		15,000

*$11,000	air filter
4,000	boiler ($5,000 depreciation x 80% used for manufacturing, as noted on the schedule)
$15,000	

The total depreciation expense in these two entries should equal the total depreciation on the schedule:

$18,000	allocated to Depreciation Expense
15,000	allocated to Inventory—Work-In-Process OH
$33,000	total depreciation taken for 2006 on the schedule

The depreciation schedule serves one more purpose. If PlatCo decides to sell or trade-in a partially depreciated asset, you must determine the asset's book value (acquisition cost – accumulated depreciation) to see if there is a gain or loss. You can find the accumulated depreciation for a particular asset on the depreciation schedule (not in Accumulated Depreciation because the balance in this account usually includes depreciation for all the assets in that group, such as Accumulated Depreciation—Vehicles). For

---

1. For an explanation of why the account Inventory—Work-In-Process OH is used, see the note on page 19.

example, suppose that PlatCo sells its van in January, 2007. A quick look at the depreciation schedule shows $8,000 accumulated depreciation for the van to date. Thus, in January, 2007, when the van is sold, the book value is $17,000. To compute: $25,000 acquisition cost (shown on the schedule as $20,000 depreciable base + $5,000 residual value) – $8,000 accumulated depreciation = $17,000 book value.

Revising the Estimated Life

It is not unusual for a company to discover that it has made an incorrect estimate for an asset's life or residual value. When this occurs, the company can revise the estimated life or the residual value and compute the new annual depreciation expense.

QUIZ 1   THE STRAIGHT-LINE METHOD OF DEPRECIATION

Problem I.

Multiple choice. Circle the correct answer.

1. The formula to compute the straight-line depreciate rate is . . .

    a. 100% ÷ residual value.
    b. 100% ÷ acquisition cost.
    c. 100% ÷ estimated life.
    d. 100% ÷ (acquisition cost – residual value).

2. Over the life of an asset, the total amount of depreciation recorded equals . . .

    a. original cost.
    b. original cost – residual value.
    c. FMV.
    d. book value.

Use the following information for Questions 3–7: Big AutoCo erects a new showroom at a cost of $1.4 million. The company expects the showroom to last for 20 years and to have a residual value of $200,000. The company uses straight-line depreciation.

3. The annual depreciation rate on the building is . . .

    a. 10%   b. 8%   c. 6%   d. 5%

4. Annual depreciation is . . .

    a. $120,000   b. $70,000   c. $60,000   d. $50,000

5. If the building is used only 4 months in the first year, depreciation for this year is . . .

    a. $46,667   b. $40,000   c. $23,333   d. $20,000

6. If the building is used only four months in the first year, depreciation in the last year will be . . .

a. $60,000   b. $40,000   c. $20,000   d. $0

7. Total depreciation over the building's estimated life is . . .

a. $1,400,000   b. $1,200,000   c. $600,000   d. $60,000

8. Under GAAP, depreciation of a newly acquired asset may not begin before the date on which . . .

a. the asset is paid for.
b. the asset has been placed in service.
c. the asset has been paid for and placed in service.
d. the buyer's fiscal year begins.

Problem II.

Use the following information to answer Questions 1–4: The invoice for the new griddle purchased by Pancake House shows $9,000 for the griddle and $1,500 for installation. The company, which uses straight-line depreciation, expects the griddle to last for 3 years and have no residual value.

1. If the griddle is purchased at the beginning of the year, what is its first-year depreciation?

2. If the griddle is installed on August 1, what is its first-year depreciation?

3. If the griddle is installed on August 1, what is its depreciation for . . .

a. Year 2?   b. Year 3?   c. Year 4?

4. Show total depreciation taken for the griddle over its estimated life.

Problem III.

On January 10, 20X1, TreeCo, which uses straight-line depreciation, and has a policy of depreciating all assets purchased between the 1st and 15th of the month as of the beginning of that month, purchases a truck for $86,000 that it estimates will last 5 years and will have no residual value. Compute the depreciation expense and the balance in Accumulated Depreciation for . . .

1. 20X1.

2. 20X2.

Problem IV.

SyCo uses straight-line depreciation and has a policy of depreciating all assets purchased between the 1st and 15th of the month as of the beginning of that month. On January 1, 20X1, SyCo purchases a computer for $14,000 that it expects to last for 4 years and have a residual value of $2,000. Use these data to complete the following table:

Year ending	Depreciation expense for the year	Credit to Accum. Depreciation	Year-end balance in Accum. Depreciation	Year-end book value
01/01/X1				
12/31/X1				
12/31/X2				
12/31/X3				
12/31/X4				

QUIZ 1 *Solutions and Explanations*

Problem I.

1. c

2. b
The original cost less residual value is equal to the depreciable base, which is the total amount of depreciation permitted for the asset over its useful life.

3. d
100% ÷ 20-year life = 5% depreciation rate

4. c
To compute: $1,400,000 original cost – $200,000 residual value = $1,200,000 depreciable base x 5% depreciation rate = $60,000 annual depreciation

5. d
To compute: $60,000 annual depreciation ÷ 12 months = $5,000 depreciation per month x 4 months = $20,000 depreciation in the first year. A faster computation is: $60,000 annual depreciation x 4/12 = $20,000.

6. b
To compute depreciation in the first year: $60,000 annual depreciation ÷ 12 months = $5,000 depreciation per month x 4 months = $20,000 (or $60,000 x $\frac{4}{12}$ = $20,000). To determine depreciation for the last year, simply subtract the $20,000 from one full year's depreciation expense as follows: $60,000 annual depreciation – $20,000 depreciation taken in the first year = $40,000 depreciation to be taken in the last year.

7. b
This is the same as the depreciable base. To compute: $1,400,000 original cost – $200,000 residual value = $1,200,000 depreciable base.

8. b

Problem II.

1. $3,500

   To compute the acquisition cost: $9,000 invoice price + $1,500 for installation = $10,500

   To compute the depreciable base: $10,500 acquisition cost – $0 residual value = $10,500

   To compute annual depreciation: $10,500 depreciable base ÷ 3 years' estimated life = $3,500

2. $3,500 annual depreciation (computed above) ÷ 12 = $291.67 x 5 months (August–December) = $1,458 rounded. (Or $3,500 x $\frac{5}{12}$ = $1,458 rounded.)

3. a. Depreciation for Year 2 is $3,500, the normal annual depreciation computed in (1) above.

   b. Depreciation for Year 3 is $3,500, the normal annual depreciation computed in (1) above.

   c. Depreciation for Year 4, the last year in the griddle's estimated life, is the depreciation not taken in Year 1. To compute: $3,500 annual depreciation – $1,458 depreciation taken for 5 months in Year 1 = $2,042 depreciation for Year 4. (You can, instead, compute depreciation for Year 3 using fractions: $3,500 x $\frac{7}{12}$* = $2,042)

   *For the 7 months of depreciation from January-July in Year 3.

4. Total depreciation taken for the griddle over its useful life is as follows:

$ 1,458	Year 1 depreciation
$ 3,500	Year 2 depreciation
$ 3,500	Year 3 depreciation
$ 2,042	Year 4 depreciation
$10,500	Total depreciation (the same amount as the depreciable base)

Problem III.

Because the truck was acquired on January 10, TruCo will depreciate it as if the purchase had been made on the 1st in keeping with company policy.

1. To compute depreciation for 20X1: $86,000 original cost – $0 salvage value = $86,000 depreciable base

$86,000 depreciable base ÷ 5 years estimated life = $17,200 annual depreciation

The entry to record this expense is as follows:

Depreciation Expense	17,200	
Accumulated Depreciation		17,200

Thus, accumulated depreciation at the end of 20X1 is $17,200.

2. In 20X2, the same entry will be made to record depreciation:

Depreciation Expense	17,200	
Accumulated Depreciation		17,200

When $17,200 is added to the Accumulated Depreciation account at the end of 20X2, it will bring total accumulated depreciation to $34,400 ($17,200 accumulated depreciation for 20X1 + $17,200 accumulated depreciation for 20X2 = $34,400).

Problem IV.

Year ending	Depreciation expense for the year	Credit to Accum. Depreciation	Year-end balance in Accum. Depreciation	Year-end book value
01/01/X1				$14,000
12/31/X1	($14,000 – $2,000) 25% = $3,000	$3,000	$ 3,000	11,000
12/31/X2	($14,000 – $2,000) 25% = $3,000	3,000	6,000	8,000
12/31/X3	($14,000 – $2,000) 25% = $3,000	3,000	9,000	5,000
12/31/X4	($14,000 – $2,000) 25% = $3,000	3,000	12,000	2,000

QUIZ 2   THE STRAIGHT-LINE METHOD OF DEPRECIATION

Problem I.

Mark each statement True or False.

1. Straight-line depreciation generally results in equal amounts of depreciation in each year.

     a. True   b. False

2. The difference between the cost of an asset and its residual value is its book value.

     a. True   b. False

3. The balance in Accumulated Depreciation decreases each year by the amount of depreciation taken.

     a. True   b. False

4. An asset is always depreciated for a full year in the year of acquisition.

     a. True   b. False

5. An asset's book value is the amount for which it can be sold.

     a. True   b. False

Problem II.

On March 1, 20X6, TyCo, which uses straight-line depreciation, pays the following invoice:

Machine	$14,000
Transportation	800
Installation	500

TyCo expects the machine, which was installed on March 1, to last for 8 years and to have a residual value of $2,000. Show annual depreciation for . . .

1. 20X6.

2. 20X7.

Problem III.

An asset is acquired on January 1, 20X1, for $350,000. It is expected to last 10 years and have a residual value of $15,000 after being depreciated under the straight-line method. Use these data to complete the following table:

Year ending	Depreciation expense for the year	Credit to Accum. Depreciation	Year-end balance in Accum. Depreciation	Year-end book value
01/01/X1				
12/31/X1				
12/31/X2				
12/31/X3				
12/31/X4				

Problem IV.

You have the following data for your company's new telecommunications system:

Cost	$35,000
Expected residual value	$ 2,500
Expected useful life	10 years

Compute the straight-line depreciation for the first year, assuming the system is acquired on . . .

1. March 1, 20X1.

2. November 1, 20X1.

Problem V.

You take on a new client who gives you the following data for a computer acquired on August 1, 20X1:

Invoice cost	$5,500
Sales tax	$ 400
Delivery charges	$ 250
Installation and programming	$ 850
Residual value	$2,000
Expected useful life	3 years

If the company uses straight-line depreciation, compute annual depreciation for . . .

1. 20X1.

2. 20X2.

QUIZ 2 *Solutions and Explanations*

Problem I.

1. True

However, if the asset had been purchased during the year, the depreciation amount may differ in the first and last years.

2. False

Book value is equal to the acquisition cost less total accumulated depreciation. The acquisition cost less the residual value is the depreciable base.

3. False

The accumulated depreciation account *increases* each year by the amount taken for depreciation.

4. False

A partial year's depreciation is taken for assets purchased during the year.

5. False

Book value represents the acquisition cost less accumulated depreciation, which is completely unrelated to the market value. To put it another way, book value is that portion of an asset's cost that has not yet been depreciated.

Problem II.

1. Annual depreciation for 20X6 is $1,386.

To compute depreciation for 20X6, you must first determine the acquisition cost and depreciable base:

$14,000	invoice price
800	transportation
500	installation
$15,300	acquisition cost

$15,300 acquisition cost – $2,000 residual value = $13,300 depreciable base

$13,300 depreciable base ÷ 8 years = $1,663 (rounded) annual depreciation x $^{10}/_{12}$ (for the 10 months from March–December) = $1,386 (rounded) depreciation for 20X6

2. Annual depreciation for 20X7 is the full year's depreciation expense of $1,663 (computed above).

Problem III.

To compute the depreciable base: $350,000 acquisition cost – $15,000 residual value = $335,000 depreciable base

To compute annual depreciation: $335,000 ÷ 10 years' estimated life – $33,500 annual depreciation expense

Year ending	Depreciation expense for the year	Credit to Accum. Depreciation	Year-end balance in Accum. Depreciation	Year-end book value
01/01/X1				$350,000
12/31/X1	$33,500	$33,500	$33,500	316,500
12/31/X2	33,500	33,500	67,000	283,000
12/31/X3	33,500	33,500	100,500	249,500
12/31/X4	33,500	33,500	134,000	216,000

Problem IV.

1. If the asset was acquired on March 1, 20X1, then straight-line depreciation for 20X1 is $2,708.

To compute the depreciable base: $35,000 acquisition cost – $2,500 residual value = $32,500 depreciable base

To compute annual depreciation: $32,500 depreciable base ÷ 10 years (estimated life) = $3,250 annual depreciation

To compute depreciation for 10 months (March-December): $3,250 x $\frac{10}{12}$ = $2,708 (rounded) depreciation for 20X1

2. If the asset was acquired on November 1, 20X1, then straight-line depreciation for 20X1 would be $542.

To compute: $3,250 annual depreciation x $\frac{2}{12}$ (for the 2 months November and December) = $542 (rounded) depreciation expense for 20X1

Problem V.

1. Depreciation at the end of 20X1 is $694.

   To compute acquisition cost:

$5,500	invoice cost
400	sales tax
250	delivery
850	installation and programming
$7,000	acquisition cost

   To compute the depreciable base: $7,000 acquisition cost
   – $2,000 residual value = $5,000 depreciable base

   To compute annual depreciation: $5,000 ÷ 3 years (estimated life)
   = $1,666.67 annual depreciation

   To compute depreciation for 5 months (August-December):
   $1,666.67 x $\frac{5}{12}$ = $694 depreciation at the end of 20X1

2. The annual depreciation for 20X2, computed above, is $1,667
   (rounded).

Section 4

THE UNITS OF PRODUCTION METHOD OF DEPRECIATION

Introduction

The units of production method depreciates an asset's cost by how many units it produces or how many hours it is used, rather than by the number of years it is in service.

For example, if your company purchases a plastic extruder, it might estimate the asset's useful life as 20,800 units rather than as, say, 10 years. This means that if the machine produces all 20,800 units in the first year, it will be fully depreciated. Or it may produce the 20,800 units over 15 or 20 years. The point is that, under the units of production (UOP) method, depreciation is not measured by the number of years that the asset is used.

Computing Depreciation Under the Units of Production Method

For most assets, units of production are measured in a number of ways, including:

- units produced

- miles driven (usually only for vehicles)

- labor or machine hours (hours used)

Management must select the appropriate category to use throughout the asset's life.

The computation for units of production depreciation is simple:

$$\frac{\text{Depreciable base}}{\text{Estimated life (in units, miles, hours, etc.)}} = \text{depreciation rate} \times \text{output for year} = \text{annual depreciation}$$

PROBLEM 1: On January 1, LiCo, which uses the units of production method, purchases* a delivery van for $10,000. Before deciding on which unit of production to use for depreciation, management estimates the vehicle's useful life in several ways, as follows:

- 30,000 hours

- 200,000 miles

- 10,000 deliveries

At the end of its useful life, LiCo expects the vehicle to have a residual value of $1,000. What is the depreciation rate for the delivery van using hours? miles? deliveries?

SOLUTION 1: First compute the depreciable base: $10,000 acquisition cost – $1,000 residual value = $9,000 depreciable base

To compute the depreciation rate based on hours used:

$$\frac{\$9,000 \text{ depreciable base}}{30,000 \text{ hours (estimated life)}} = \$0.30 \text{ (per hour) depreciation rate}$$

To compute the depreciation rate using the number of miles driven:

$$\frac{\$9,000 \text{ depreciable base}}{200,000 \text{ miles driven (estimated life)}} = \$0.045 \text{ (per mile) depreciation rate}$$

To compute the depreciation rate using the deliveries made:

$$\frac{\$9,000 \text{ depreciable base}}{10,000 \text{ deliveries (estimated life)}} = \$0.90 \text{ (per delivery) depreciation rate}$$

After LiCo selects the measure it will use (hours used, miles driven or deliveries made), it will compute annual depreciation for the vehicle by multiplying the number of units of output by this rate.

---

*Under both generally accepted accounting principles (GAAP) and tax law, depreciation cannot begin until the asset has been acquired *and* placed in service. However, to avoid cumbersome, repetitious language ("acquires and places in service . . ."), it is assumed throughout this course that the acquired asset is placed in service on the date of purchase.

PROBLEM 2: Use the data from the previous problem and solution to answer the following questions:

1. LiCo decides to measure the vehicle's life in hours used, as follows:

Year 1	3,100 hours used
Year 2	2,950 hours used

Show annual depreciation and the adjusting journal entry to record it for Year 1 and Year 2.

2. LiCo decides to measure the vehicle's life in miles driven, as follows:

Year 1	21,000 miles
Year 2	22,500 miles

Show annual depreciation and the adjusting journal entry to record it for Year 1 and Year 2.

3. LiCo decides to measure the vehicle's life in deliveries, as follows:

Year 1	1,500 deliveries
Year 2	1,350 deliveries

Show annual depreciation and the adjusting journal entry to record it for Year 1 and Year 2.

SOLUTION 2: Use the depreciation rates computed in Solution 1 for each answer.

1. To compute annual depreciation using the depreciation rate of $0.30 (per hour used):

<u>For Year 1</u>
3,100 hours used x $0.30 depreciation rate = $930 annual depreciation

Depreciation Expense	930	
Accumulated Depreciation		930

<u>For Year 2</u>
2,950 hours used x $0.30 depreciation rate = $885 depreciation rate.

Depreciation Expense	885	
Accumulated Depreciation		885

2. To compute annual depreciation using the depreciation rate of $0.045 (per mile driven):

<u>For Year 1</u>
21,000 miles driven x $0.045 depreciation rate = $945 annual depreciation

Depreciation Expense	945	
Accumulated Depreciation		945

<u>For Year 2</u>
22,500 miles driven x $0.045 depreciation rate = $1,013 (rounded) annual depreciation

Depreciation Expense	1,013	
Accumulated Depreciation		1,013

3. To compute annual depreciation using the depreciation rate of $0.90 (per delivery made):

<u>For Year 1</u>
1,500 deliveries x $0.90 depreciation rate = $1,350 annual depreciation

Depreciation Expense	1,350	
Accumulated Depreciation		1,350

<u>For Year 2</u>
1,350 deliveries x $0.90 depreciation rate = $1,215 annual depreciation

Depreciation Expense	1,215	
Accumulated Depreciation		1,215

PROBLEM 3: MyCo, which uses units of production depreciation, acquires equipment and pays the following invoice:

Equipment	$20,000
Sales tax	1,600
Freight	1,400

MyCo estimates that the equipment will produce 30,000 units over its life and will have a residual value of $2,000 at the end of that time.

Compute annual depreciation for the first 2 years, and show the adjusting entry to record depreciation expense if MyCo produces 6,200 units in Year 1 and 5,800 units in Year 2.

SOLUTION 3: Before MyCo can compute depreciation, it must determine the depreciable base:

$20,000	equipment
1,600	sales tax
1,400	freight
$23,000	acquisition cost
(2,000)	residual value
$21,000	depreciable base

Next, MyCo computes the depreciation rate:

$$\frac{\$21,000 \text{ depreciable base}}{30,000 \text{ units (estimated life)}} = \$0.70 \text{ (per unit) depreciation rate}$$

Now MyCo can compute annual depreciation for Year 1 and Year 2 as follows:

For Year 1
6,200 units produced x $0.70 depreciation rate = $4,340 depreciation

Depreciation Expense	4,340	
Accumulated Depreciation		4,340

For Year 2
5,800 units x $0.70 depreciation rate = $4,060 depreciation

Depreciation Expense	4,060	
Accumulated Depreciation		4,060

PROBLEM 4: MyCo, from Problem 3, decides to base its units of production depreciation on machine hours instead of units produced and estimates that the equipment will last for 40,000 hours. Compute annual depreciation for the first 2 years and show the adjusting entry to record depreciation expense if MyCo uses the equipment 10,500 hours in Year 1 and 12,000 hours in Year 2, and computes the depreciation rate to three places ($0.000).

SOLUTION 4: The depreciable base was computed at $22,000 in Solution 2.

To compute the depreciation rate using labor hours:

$$\frac{\$21,000 \text{ depreciable base}}{40,000 \text{ labor hours (estimated life)}} = \$0.525 \text{ (per hour) depreciation rate}$$

For Year 1
10,500 hours x $0.525 depreciation rate = $5,513 depreciation (rounded)

Depreciation Expense	5,513	
Accumulated Depreciation		5,513

For Year 2
12,000 hours x $0.525 depreciation rate = $6,300

Depreciation Expense	6,300	
Accumulated Depreciation		6,300

When Assets Are Acquired During the Year

Under the units of production method, the time of year when the asset is purchased is irrelevant to first-year depreciation — or the depreciation in any other year—because the computation is based only on the number of units produced, hours used, miles driven, etc. The date of purchase does not matter. For example, an asset is purchased on January 1 and produces 150,000 units in the first year. Depreciation expense for the year will be the same whether all the units are produced on January 1, December 31 or at any other time during the year.

PROBLEM 5: On June 1, BarCo acquires equipment with an acquisition cost of $100,000. Management expects the equipment to produce 2,000,000 units and to have a residual value of $10,000. What is the depreciation rate?

SOLUTION 5: To compute: $100,000 acquisition cost – $10,000 residual value = $90,000 depreciable base ÷ 2,000,000 units (estimated life) = $0.045 (per unit) depreciation rate

PROBLEM 6: Assume the same facts as in Problem 5, but with the following output:

Year	Units produced	Year	Units produced
Year 1	123,000	Year 7	193,000
Year 2	225,000	Year 8	186,000
Year 3	208,000	Year 9	185,000
Year 4	206,000	Year 10	178,000
Year 5	209,000	Year 11	87,000
Year 6	200,000		

What is the annual depreciation, accumulated depreciation and book value in each year of the asset's life?

SOLUTION 6: The following table illustrates the annual depreciation, accumulated depreciation and book value in each year of the asset's life:

Year ending	Depreciation expense for the year	Credit to Accum. Depreciation	Year-end balance in Accum. Depreciation	Year-end book value
6/01/X1				$100,000*
12/31/X1	123,000 x $.045 = $ 5,535	$ 5,535	$ 5,535	94,465
12/31/X2	225,000 x $.045 = 10,125	10,125	15,660	84,340
12/31/X3	208,000 x $.045 = 9,360	9,360	25,020	74,980
12/31/X4	206,000 x $.045 = 9,270	9,270	34,290	65,710
12/31/X5	209,000 x $.045 = 9,405	9,405	43,695	56,305
12/31/X6	200,000 x $.045 = 9,000	9,000	52,695	47,305
12/31/X7	193,000 x $.045 = 8,685	8,685	61,380	38,620
12/31/X8	186,000 x $.045 = 8,370	8,370	69,750	30,250
12/31/X9	185,000 x $.045 = 8,325	8,325	78,075	21,925
12/31/X10	178,000 x $.045 = 8,010	8,010	86,085	13,915
12/31/X11	87,000 x $.045 = 3,915	3,915	90,000	10,000

*Acquisition cost and initial book value. Beneath this amount is the book value (original cost – accumulated depreciation) at the end of each year.

At the end of each year, the balance in the accumulated depreciation account increases and the book value decreases. Total depreciation over the asset's 2,000,000-unit life is $90,000, the same amount as the depreciable base. At the end of the asset's life, the book value of $10,000 ($100,000 acquisition cost – $90,000 total accumulated depreciation) equals the residual value.

No example is given to show depreciation if the asset was purchased on June 30 because depreciation is unrelated to date of purchase. As long as

123,000 units are produced in the first year, depreciation is $5,535 whether the machine is purchased on January 1, June 30, or any other date.

Completing the Depreciation Schedule at Year End

The example of PlatCo, a manufacturer of dishware that prepares its financial statements under generally accepted accounting principles (GAAP), is continued here from Section 3. There is no need to refer to that section; the relevant data are provided here.

During 2007, PlatCo acquires the following assets, which it will depreciate under the units of production depreciation method:

- On February 17, PlatCo acquires a water purifier for the company for $75,000 plus $3,750 sales tax, $250 freight and $1,000 for installation. PlatCo estimates that the equipment will purify 1.3 million gallons over its useful life, of which 70% will be for the factory and 30% for the offices, and that it will have a residual value of $15,000. During 2007, the equipment purifies 150,000 gallons.

- On June 30, PlatCo buys a used Dodge delivery van for $13,500 but must install a new transmission for $1,500 to make it ready for use. PlatCo estimates that the pickup will haul 10,000 cartons of cookware to the local freight center over its useful life and will have a residual value of $7,000. During 2007, the Dodge van is used to haul 2,300 cartons.

- On December 20, PlatCo acquires a used plastic extruder for $120,000, including taxes and installation, that it estimates will pump out 1,000,000 tops for its dishware containers and will have a residual value of $30,000. During the last week of the year, the machine pumps out 10,000 tops.

On pages 68–69 are photocopies of PlatCo's 2006 depreciation schedule, which is already full, and a blank copy of the schedule that PlatCo must complete for 2007. Complete the 2007 schedule by continuing to depreciate all assets that PlatCo is depreciating under the straight-line (SL) method, and adding the new assets acquired by PlatCo in 2007 that the company will depreciate under units of production. Check your work against the completed schedule on page 70.

Before you can complete the schedule for 2007, you need to compute 2007 depreciation expense for the various assets. Try to do these computations before looking at how they are done below.

To compute 2007 depreciation for the water purifier:
$75,000 cost + $3,750 sales tax + $250 freight + $1,000 installation =
$80,000 acquisition cost – $15,000 residual value = $65,000 depreciable base
÷ 1,300,000 gallons (estimated life) = $0.05 (per gallon) depreciation rate
x 150,000 gallons purified in 2007 = $7,500 depreciation expense for 2007

To compute 2007 depreciation for the Dodge van:
$13,500 cost + $1,500 transmission to make the pickup ready for use =
$15,000 acquisition cost – $7,000 residual value = $8,000 depreciable base
÷ 10,000 cartons (estimated life) = $0.80 (per carton hauled) depreciation rate
x 2,300 (cartons hauled in 2007) = $1,840 depreciation expense for 2007

To compute 2007 depreciation for the plastic extruder:
$120,000 acquisition cost – $30,000 residual value = $90,000 depreciable base
÷ 1,000,000 tops (estimated life) = $0.09 (per plastic top) depreciation rate
x 10,000 tops = $900 depreciation expense for 2007

Depreciation Schedule (2006)

Methods
SL = straight-line
DB = declining balance
SYD = sum-of-the-years'-digits

KIND OF PROPERTY	DATE ACQUIRED	METHOD	RATE OR LIFE	DEPRECIABLE COST OR OTHER BASIS	RESIDUAL (SALVAGE) VALUE	DEPRECIATION IN PRIOR YEARS	DEPRECIATION FOR YR. ENDED 12/31/04	ACCUMULATED DEPRECIATION 12/31/04	DEPRECIATION FOR YR. ENDED 12/31/05	ACCUMULATED DEPRECIATION 12/31/05	DEPRECIATION FOR YR. ENDED 12/31/06	ACCUMULATED DEPRECIATION 12/31/06
Property												
Office Building	1/5/00	SL	30 yrs	300,000	100,000	40,000	10,000	50,000	10,000	60,000	10,000	70,000
Land for ofc. bldg.	1/5/00	NA		55,000								
Warehouse	11/12/72	SL	4%	90,000	25,000	90,000		90,000		90,000		90,000
Land for warehouse	11/12/72	NA		32,000								
Equipment												
Boiler (80% man.)	1/1/01	SL	15 yrs	75,000	10,000	15,000	5,000	20,000	5,000	25,000	5,000	30,000
Air filter (100% man.)	7/2/03	SL	8 yrs	88,000	5,000	5,500	11,000	16,500	11,000	27,500	11,000	38,500
Vehicles _Sold 1/30/06_												
Chevrolet Nova	1/1/00	SL	5 yrs	15,000	3,000	12,000	3,000	15,000	-0-	15,000	SOLD	
Oldsmobile	11/3/04	SL	6 yrs	18,000	6,000		500	500	3,000	3,500	3,000	6,500
Delivery van (used)	1/14/05	SL	20%	20,000	5,000				4,000	4,000	4,000	8,000
Totals				693,000	154,000	162,500	29,500	192,000	33,000	210,000	33,000	243,000

Depreciation Schedule (2007)

Methods
SL = straight-line
DB = declining balance
SYD = sum-of-the-years'-digits

KIND OF PROPERTY	DATE ACQUIRED	METHOD	RATE OR LIFE	DEPRECIABLE COST OR OTHER BASIS	RESIDUAL (SALVAGE) VALUE	DEPRECIATION IN PRIOR YEARS	DEPRECIATION FOR YR. ENDED	ACCUMULATED DEPRECIATION	DEPRECIATION FOR YR. ENDED	ACCUMULATED DEPRECIATION	DEPRECIATION FOR YR. ENDED	ACCUMULATED DEPRECIATION

Depreciation Schedule (2007)

Methods
SL = straight line
DB = declining balance
SYD = sum-of-the-years' digits

KIND OF PROPERTY	DATE ACQUIRED	METHOD	RATE OR LIFE	DEPRECIABLE COST OR OTHER BASIS	RESIDUAL (SALVAGE) VALUE	DEPRECIATION IN PRIOR YEARS	DEPRECIATION FOR YR. ENDED 12/31/07	ACCUMULATED DEPRECIATION 12/31/07	DEPRECIATION FOR YR. ENDED	ACCUMULATED DEPRECIATION	DEPRECIATION FOR YR. ENDED	ACCUMULATED DEPRECIATION
Property												
Office Building	1/5/00	SL	30 yrs	300,000	100,000	70,000	10,000	80,000				
Land for ofc. bldg.	1/5/00	NA		55,000								
Warehouse	11/12/72	SL	4%	90,000	25,000	90,000		90,000				
Land for warehouse	11/12/72	NA		32,000								
Equipment												
Boiler (80% man.)	1/1/01	SL	15 yrs	75,000	10,000	30,000	5,000	35,000				
Air filter (100% man.)	7/2/03	SL	8 yrs	88,000	5,000	38,500	11,000	49,500				
Water pur. (70% man.)	2/17/07	UOP	$.05/gal.	65,000	15,000		7,500	7,500				
Extruder (100% man.)	12/20/07	UOP	$.09/unit	90,000	30,000		900	900				
Vehicles												
Oldsmobile	11/3/04	SL	6 yrs	18,000	6,000	6,500	3,000	9,500				
Delivery van (used)	1/14/05	SL	20%	20,000	5,000	8,000	4,000	12,000				
Dodge van (used)	6/30/07	UOP	$.80/ctn.	8,000	7,000		1,840	1,840				
Totals				841,000	203,000	243,000	43,240	286,240				

Notes on the depreciation schedule:

- The newly acquired assets, purifier, extruder and Dodge van are shown on the depreciation schedule in boldface type

- 2007 depreciation expense and accumulated depreciation are shown on the depreciation schedule in boldface type

- Land included in the purchase of the office building and warehouse is presented on the schedule even though it is not depreciated because most firms show *all* assets on their depreciation schedule.

- Although the warehouse was fully depreciated years ago, PlatCo continues to present this and every other asset the company owns on the depreciation schedule until the asset is disposed of.

- Assets used partly or entirely for manufacturing show the percentage of use allocated to manufacturing next to them so that anyone who reads the schedule will be able to make the year-end adjusting entries correctly. This is one of many ways to show the allocation.

- The Chevrolet Nova does not appear on the 2007 schedule because PlatCo sold (disposed of) it in 2006.

In computing depreciation for PlatCo, you would take the following steps to make sure that all of PlatCo's assets had been depreciated in 2007:

1. Total the depreciable cost column, then total the residual value column. Add the totals from the two columns to yield the total acquisition cost of all assets that PlatCo is depreciating in 2007. To compute:

$ 841,000	total "depreciable cost or other basis" of all assets on the depreciation schedule
+ 203,000	total residual value of all assets on the depreciation schedule
$1,044,000	total acquisition cost of all assets on the depreciation schedule

2. Subtract the acquisition cost of any assets on the 2007 schedule that were sold before 2007. Because no assets on this schedule were sold, the total acquisition cost of all assets on the depreciation schedule is $1,044,000.

3. To verify the schedule, go to the general ledger, find all plant and equipment asset accounts and total the balances (each balance is an asset's acquisition cost). The total should be $1,044,000. If the total of all depreciable asset account balances is more than $1,044,000, then somewhere there is another asset that PlatCo has omitted. If the total is less than $1,044,000, then the schedule may list an asset that the company no longer owns, or there may be an error.

By including land on the depreciation schedule, you can quickly check the schedule against the general ledger asset accounts. If land had been left off the schedule, you would have to add the balances of only the *depreciable* accounts, increasing the likelihood of errors and undermining the crosscheck.

Two adjusting entries are required to record PlatCo's depreciation expense for 2007. The first entry allocates depreciation for nonmanufacturing assets to the Depreciation Expense account. This entry will include depreciation for most of the depreciable assets.

The data that you need to allocate depreciation for the water purifier, extruder and Dodge van were given with the information describing the three purchases on page 66.

The data that you need to compute depreciation for the air filter and boiler were given in Section 3 and are repeated here. The air filter is used 100% by the factory. The boiler is used 80% by the factory and 20% by the offices.

The first entry records depreciation to Depreciation Expense:

Depreciation Expense	22,090*	
Accumulated Depreciation—Buildings		10,000
Accumulated Depreciation—Equipment		3,250**
Accumulated Depreciation—Vehicles		8,840

*$10,000	office building
1,000	boiler ($5,000 depreciation x 20% office use as noted on the schedule)
2,250	water purifier ($7,500 depreciation x 30% office use as noted on the schedule)
3,000	Oldsmobile
4,000	delivery van
1,840	Dodge van (a selling expense and therefore not part of work-in-process overhead [OH])
$22,090	

**$1,000 boiler + $2,250 water purifier

The second entry allocates depreciation to the Inventory—Work-In-Process OH[1] account:

Inventory—Work-In-Process OH	21,150*
Accumulated Depreciation—Equipment	21,150

*$ 4,000	boiler ($5,000 depreciation x 80% used for manufacturing as noted on the schedule)
11,000	air filter (100% used for manufacturing as noted on the schedule)
5,250	water purifier ($7,500 depreciation x 70% used for manufacturing as noted on the schedule)
900	plastic extruder (100% used for manufacturing as noted on the schedule)
$21,150	

The total depreciation expense in these two entries should equal total depreciation on the schedule. To compute:

$22,090	allocated to Depreciation Expense
21,150	allocated to Inventory—Work-In-Process OH
$43,240	total depreciation taken for 2007 on the schedule

If PlatCo decides to sell or trade in a depreciable asset, you must bring the accumulated depreciation up to date as of the date of disposal. In the Accumulated Depreciation account, you will find total depreciation for *all* buildings, or *all* equipment or *all* vehicles, rather than for the particular asset that was disposed of. But on the depreciation schedule, you will find total depreciation for each asset as of the end of the prior year. Simply add accumulated depreciation taken in the current year to find total accumulated depreciation to date.

Revising the Estimated Life

It is not unusual for a company to discover that it has made an incorrect estimate of an asset's life or residual value. When this occurs, the company can revise the estimated life or the residual value and compute the new annual depreciation expense.

---

1. For an explanation of why the account Inventory—Work-In-Process OH is used, see the note on page 19.

QUIZ 1   THE UNITS OF PRODUCTION METHOD OF DEPRECIATION

NOTE: Where journal entries are required, it is sufficient to use the account title "Accumulated Depreciation." You are not required to add a description such as "Accumulated Depreciation—Equipment" because different companies use different descriptive words. If the answer uses the account Accumulated Depreciation—Equipment, but you used Accumulated Depreciation, take full credit.

Problem I.

Mark each statement True or False.

1. The units of production method produces the same annual depreciation each year.

    a. True   b. False

2. Units of production depreciation is based on how much an asset is used, regardless of how long it is owned.

    a. True   b. False

3. In units of production, the depreciation rate remains unchanged throughout the asset's life.

    a. True   b. False

4. Under units of production depreciation, an asset's use can be measured in hours or years.

    a. True   b. False

5. Total depreciation over an asset's life is the same under units of production or straight-line depreciation.

    a. True   b. False

Problem II.

At the beginning of the year, Middlestate Farmers Cooperative, which processes and packs carrots for members, purchases for $8,500 a new conveyer that it will depreciate under the units of production method. The equipment is expected to process 60,000 pounds of carrots and have a residual value of $1,000.

1. What is the depreciation rate?

2. If Middlestate processes 18,000 pounds of carrots in the first year, what is first-year depreciation?

3. If this were Middlestate's only asset, what adjusting journal entry would it record at the end of the first year?

Problem III.

Manufacture Inc., which uses units of production depreciation, shows the following data for three pieces of equipment used in production:

Equipment	Acquisition cost	Residual value	Estimated life
Forklift	$35,000	$ 0	140,000 miles
Lathe	17,000	2,000	15,000 machine hours
Oven	8,500	500	400,000 units of output

1. If the forklift is driven 13,200 miles during 20X1, compute first-year depreciation and show the adjusting entry to record depreciation.

2. If the lathe is used 3,000 machine hours in 20X1, compute first-year depreciation and show the adjusting entry to record depreciation.

3. If the oven produces 85,000 units during 20X1, compute first-year depreciation and show the adjusting entry to record depreciation.

Problem IV.

On January 1, 20X1, Myrtle's Tree Service acquires a new truck for $80,000. Taxes, title and delivery charges are $6,000. The truck is expected to be driven 172,000 miles over its life and will have no residual value at that point. Show annual depreciation and the balance in Accumulated Depreciation for:

1. 20X1 when the truck is driven 18,000 miles.

2. 20X2 when the truck is driven 20,000 miles.

Problem V.

On January 1, 20X1, Textiles, Inc., a manufacturer that uses units of production depreciation, purchases for $14,000 a machine that will produce 16,000 yards of fabric over its life and that will end up with a residual value of $2,000. Use the following data to complete the table below. Then answer the questions below the table.

Year	Yards produced
20X1	3,500
20X2	3,428
20X3	3,212
20X4	2,948

Year ending	Depreciation expense for the year	Credit to Accum. Depreciation	Year-end balance in Accum. Depreciation	Year-end book value
01/01/X1				
12/31/X1				
12/31/X2				
12/31/X3				
12/31/X4				

1. What is the book value as of 12/31/X4?

2. How much depreciation can Textiles, Inc. take in 20X5 and subsequent years?

3. How many more yards of cloth can the machine produce after 12/31/X4 before it is fully depreciated?

QUIZ 1   Solutions and Explanations

Problem I.

1. False
The amount of depreciation varies with the asset's usage.

2. True

3. True

4. False
The depreciation rate can be measured in hours of use, but not in years (because years represent length of ownership rather than usage).

5. True

Problem II.

1. To compute the depreciation rate for the equipment based on pounds of carrots processed:

$$\frac{\$7,500^* \text{ depreciable base}}{60,000 \text{ lbs. (estimated life)}} = \$0.125 \text{ (per pound of carrots processed) depreciation rate}$$

*$8,500 cost – $1,000 residual value = $7,500 depreciable base

2. To compute first-year depreciation under units of production depreciation if 18,000 pounds of carrots are processed:

18,000 lbs. x $0.125 depreciation rate = $2,250 depreciation for the first year

3.

Inventory—Work-In-Process OH	2,250	
Accumulated Depreciation—Equipment		2,250

Because the conveyer belt is used only for the production of inventory, 100% of annual depreciation must be allocated to Inventory—Work-In-Process OH rather than to Depreciation Expense.

Problem III.

1. The first step is to compute the depreciation rate:

$35,000 cost – $0 residual value = $35,000 depreciable base

$$\frac{\$35{,}000 \text{ depreciable base}}{140{,}000 \text{ miles (estimated life)}} \quad = \quad \$0.25 \text{ (per mile) depreciation rate}$$

Once the depreciation rate is computed, you can determine first-year depreciation:

13,200 miles driven during 20X1 x $0.25 depreciation rate = $3,300 first-year depreciation

To record first-year depreciation expense:

Inventory—Work-In-Process OH	3,300	
Accumulated Depreciation—Equipment		3,300

2. To compute the depreciable base for the lathe:

$17,000 cost – $2,000 residual value = $15,000 depreciable base

$$\frac{\$15{,}000 \text{ depreciable base}}{15{,}000 \text{ hours (estimated life)}} \quad = \quad \$1 \text{ (per machine hour) depreciation rate}$$

To determine first-year depreciation:

3,000 hours x $1 depreciation rate = $3,000 depreciation

To record depreciation expense for the first year:

Inventory—Work-In-Process OH	3,000	
Accumulated Depreciation—Equipment		3,000

3. To compute the depreciation rate:

$8,500 cost – $500 residual value = $8,000 depreciable base

$$\frac{\$8,000 \text{ depreciable base}}{400,000 \text{ items output (estimated life)}} = \$0.02 \text{ (per item) depreciation rate}$$

To compute first-year depreciation:

85,000 items x $0.02 depreciation rate = $1,700 first-year depreciation

To record first-year depreciation:

Inventory—Work-In-Process OH	1,700	
Accumulated Depreciation—Equipment		1,700

Problem IV.

Before annual depreciation can be computed, you must determine the depreciable base and the depreciation rate:

$80,000	invoice cost
+6,000	taxes, title and delivery
$86,000	acquisition cost
– 0	residual value
$86,000	depreciable base

To compute the depreciation rate:

$$\frac{\$86,000 \text{ depreciable base}}{172,000 \text{ miles (estimated life)}} = \$0.50 \text{ (per mile) depreciation rate}$$

1. To compute annual depreciation for 20X1:

18,000 miles driven x $0.50 depreciation rate = $9,000 depreciation for 20X1

Because the truck was acquired in 20X1, the amount of accumulated depreciation recorded at year end would also be the balance in Accumulated Depreciation:

Depreciation Expense	9,000	
Accumulated Depreciation—Vehicles		9,000

The balance in Accumulated Depreciation is the same as annual depreciation for 20X1: $9,000.

2. To compute annual depreciation for 20X2:

20,000 miles x $0.50 depreciation rate = $10,000 annual depreciation for 20X2

Recording depreciation will add $10,000 to the balance in Accumulated Depreciation, as follows:

Depreciation Expense	10,000	
Accumulated Depreciation—Vehicles		10,000

This will leave a balance in Accumulated Depreciation of $19,000 at the end of 20X2, as the following T-account shows:

Accumulated Depreciation

9,000 bal. Dec. 31, 20X1
10,000 Dec. 31, 20X2
19,000 bal. Dec. 31, 20X2

Problem V.

To complete the table, you need to compute the depreciation rate and the depreciation for each year. To compute the depreciation rate:

$14,000 cost – $2,000 residual value = $12,000 depreciable base ÷ 16,000 yards = $0.75 depreciation rate

Year ending	Depreciation expense for the year	Credit to Accum. Depreciation	Year-end balance in Accum. Depreciation	Year-end book value
01/01/X1				$14,000
12/31/X1	3,500 x $.75 = $2,625	$2,625	$2,625	11,375
12/31/X2	3,428 x $.75 = $2,571	2,571	5,196	8,804
12/31/X3	3,212 x $.75 = $2,409	2,409	7,605	6,395
12/31/X4	2,948 x $.75 = $2,211	2,211	9,816	4,184

1. The book value as of 12/31/X4 is $4,184.

2. In 20X5 and subsequent years, Textiles, Inc. can still take $2,184 in depreciation. To compute: $12,000 depreciable base – $9,816 total depreciation (year-end balance in Accumulated Depreciation) taken through 12/31 = $2,184

3. After 12/31/X4, the machine can produce 2,912 yards of cloth before it is fully depreciated ($2,184 remaining depreciation ÷ $0.75 depreciation rate = 2,912)

QUIZ 2   THE UNITS OF PRODUCTION METHOD OF DEPRECIATION

NOTE: Where journal entries are required, it is sufficient to use the account title "Accumulated Depreciation." You are not required to add a description such as "Accumulated Depreciation—Equipment" because different companies use different descriptive words. If the answer uses the account Accumulated Depreciation—Equipment, but you used Accumulated Depreciation, take full credit.

Problem I.

Multiple choice. Circle the correct answer.

1. Under the units of production method, the depreciation rate is computed as . . .

   a. $\dfrac{\text{cost} - \text{residual value}}{\text{estimated life in years}}$

   b. $\dfrac{\text{cost} - \text{residual value}}{\text{book value}}$

   c. $\dfrac{\text{cost} - \text{residual value}}{\text{estimated life in units produced}}$

   d. $\dfrac{\text{units produced}}{\text{estimated life in years}}$

2. Over the life of an asset, total depreciation always equals . . .

   a. the book value.
   b. the depreciable base.
   c. the acquisition cost.
   d. the residual value.

Use the following information for Questions 3–5: CorpCo, which uses units of production depreciation, installs a water purifier for $15,000 that it expects to purify 64,000 gallons of water, at which point it will have a residual value of $3,000. When CorpCo computes the depreciation rate under the UOP method, it rounds to four places ($0.0000).

3. The depreciation rate (per gallon) is . . .

    a. $0.2344 (rounded)
    b. $0.2813 (rounded)
    c. $0.1875
    d. none of the above

4. If the unit processes 2,943 gallons during the year, depreciation will be ...

    a. $689 (rounded)
    b. $2,943
    c. $552 (rounded)
    d. $856 (rounded)

5. Total depreciation to be recorded over the purifier's useful life is ...

    a. $15,000
    b. $12,000
    c. $18,000
    d. $64,000

Problem II.

TileCo, which uses units of production depreciation, acquires equipment for $85,000. Management is considering two ways to record depreciation: based on machine hours, estimated at 16,000; or based on units produced, estimated at 10,000. The equipment will have a residual value of $5,000.

1. If TileCo decides to use machine hours and the equipment is run 5,800 hours during the year, how much will depreciation be for the year?

2. If TileCo decides to use units produced and the equipment outputs 2,500 units during the year, how much will depreciation be for the year?

Problem III.

On January 14, 20X1, DayCo, which uses units of production depreciation, acquires a new auto for $24,000 plus $3,000 for special features. Taxes, title and delivery are $4,000. Management estimates that the auto will be driven 150,000 miles over its life and will end up with a residual value of $1,000. Complete the following depreciation schedules, assuming the car is driven 23,000 miles in 20X1, 18,000 in 20X2 and 21,000 miles in 20X3.

Year ending	Depreciation expense for the year	Credit to Accum. Depreciation	Year-end balance in Accum. Depreciation	Year-end book value
12/31/X1				
12/31/X2				
12/31/X3				

Problem IV.

You have the following data for a machine that produces videotapes:

Cost	$35,650
Estimated residual value	$ 2,500
Estimated life	390,000 copies

Compute the depreciation for each of the following years, using a depreciation rate that goes to three places ($0.000):

1. 20X1   37,000 copies

2. 20X2   48,000 copies

QUIZ 2   Solutions and Explanations

Problem I.

1. c

2. b

3. c

To compute: $15,000 acquisition cost − $3,000 residual value = $12,000 depreciable base ÷ 64,000 gallons (estimated life) = $0.1875 depreciation rate

4. c

2,943 gallons purified x $0.1875 depreciation rate (computed in No. 3 above) = $552 (rounded) depreciation for the year

5. b

$12,000 is the amount of the depreciable base.

Problem II.

1. Before depreciation for any year can be determined, you must compute the depreciable base and depreciation rate, as follows:

To compute the depreciable base: $85,000 acquisition cost − $5,000 residual value = $80,000 depreciable base

To compute the depreciation rate:

$$\frac{\$80,000 \text{ depreciable base}}{16,000 \text{ machine hours (estimated life)}} = \$5.00 \text{ (per machine hour) depreciation rate}$$

5,800 hours x $5.00 depreciation rate = $29,000 depreciation for the year

2. To compute the depreciation rate:

$$\frac{\$80,000 \text{ depreciable base}}{10,000 \text{ units (estimated life)}} = \$8 \text{ (per unit) depreciation rate}$$

To compute annual depreciation:

2,500 items output x $8 depreciation rate = $20,000 depreciation for the year

Problem III.

Under units of production depreciation, the January 14 acquisition date is irrelevant; only usage determines depreciation. To compute the depreciable base:

$24,000	invoice cost
3,000	dealer add-ons
4,000	taxes, title and delivery
$31,000	acquisition cost
−1,000	residual value
$30,000	depreciable base

To compute the depreciation rate:

$$\frac{\$30,000 \text{ depreciable base}}{150,000 \text{ miles (estimated life)}} = \$0.20 \text{ (per mile) depreciation rate}$$

Year ending	Depreciation expense for the year	Credit to Accum. Depreciation	Year-end balance in Accum. Depreciation	Year-end book value
X1	23,000 x $.20 = $4,600	$4,600	$4,600	$26,400
X2	18,000 x $.20 = 3,600	3,600	8,200	22,800
X3	21,000 x $.20 = 4,200	4,200	12,400	18,600

Problem IV.

Before you can compute depreciation, you must compute the depreciable base and the depreciation rate, as follows: $35,650 acquisition cost – $2,500 residual value = $33,150 depreciable base

$$\frac{\$33{,}150 \text{ depreciable base}}{390{,}000 \text{ video copies (estimated life)}} = \$0.085 \text{ (per copy) depreciation rate (rounded)}$$

1. To compute annual depreciation for 20X1:

37,000 videos x $0.085 depreciation rate = $3,145 depreciation for 20X1

2. To compute annual depreciation for 20X2:

48,000 videos x $0.085 depreciation rate = $4,080 depreciation for 20X2

Section 5
THE DECLINING BALANCE METHOD OF DEPRECIATION

Introduction

Sometimes a company knows that an asset will be more efficient in its early years than in its later years. For example, computerized equipment may be used extensively when first acquired, then either quickly become obsolete or be used much less when more advanced equipment becomes available.

The solution is to use a depreciation method that provides most of the depreciation in the early years of use and less in later years. Two methods that accelerate depreciation are the *declining balance* (DB) method, covered in this section, and the sum-of-the-years'-digits (SYD) method, covered in Section 6.

Calculating Depreciation
Under the Declining Balance Method

The depreciation *rate* for the DB method is a multiple of the straight-line (SL) rate. Although any percentage may be used, the most common declining balance rates are:

- 200%—2 x straight-line rate;

- 150%—1.5 x straight-line rate; or

- 125%—1.25 x straight-line rate.

The most widely used rate is 200%, referred to as the *double-declining balance* (DDB) method because it is double the straight-line rate. Whatever rate a company selects—200%, 150%, 125%, or another rate—must be used over the entire life of the asset.

How Depreciation Is Computed Under the Declining Balance Method

The DB method is different from the SL, units of production (UOP) or sum-of-the-years'-digits methods because the depreciation rate is multiplied by the *book value*, not the depreciable base. Because the book value declines each year, it is called the declining balance method.

To compute depreciation expense under DDB, multiply the depreciation rate by the book value—*not* the depreciable cost as in the straight-line and units of production methods. The total depreciation permitted for an asset, however, is limited to the depreciable base as in the other methods. To put it another way, the asset cannot be depreciated below its residual value, as in the other methods.

EXAMPLE 1: On January 1, GruCo, which uses the DDB method, purchases* a machine with an acquisition cost of $75,000, an estimated life of 5 years and a residual value of $5,000. GruCo depreciates the machine as follows:

To determine the depreciation rate:

$$\frac{1.00}{5 \text{ years (estimated life)}} = 20\% \text{ straight-line rate x } 200\% = 40\% \text{ DDB rate}$$

To compute depreciation for Year 1:
$75,000 book value x 40% = $30,000 depreciation

The journal entry to record depreciation in Year 1 is:

Depreciation Expense	30,000	
Accumulated Depreciation—Equipment		30,000

To compute the book value at the end of Year 1:
$75,000 acquisition cost − $30,000 accumulated depreciation = $45,000 book value

---

*Under both generally accepted accounting principles (GAAP) and tax law, depreciation cannot begin until the asset has been acquired *and* placed in service. However, to avoid cumbersome, repetitious language ("acquires and places in service . . ."), it is assumed throughout this course that the acquired asset is placed in service on the date of purchase.

<u>To compute depreciation for Year 2</u>:
40% depreciation rate x $45,000 book value* (*not* depreciable base) =
$18,000 depreciation

* $75,000 cost – $30,000 Year 1 depreciation

The journal entry to record depreciation in Year 2 is:

Depreciation Expense	18,000	
Accumulated Depreciation—Equipment		18,000

<u>To compute the book value at the end of Year 2</u>:
$75,000 acquisition cost – $48,000* accumulated depreciation =
$27,000 book value.

*$30,000 depreciation from Year 1 + $18,000 depreciation from Year 2.

<u>To compute depreciation for Year 3</u>:
40% depreciation rate x $27,000 book value (*not* depreciable base) =
$10,800 depreciation

The journal entry to record depreciation in Year 3 is:

Depreciation Expense	10,800	
Accumulated Depreciation—Equipment		10,800

The asset will be depreciated until the book value equals the residual value, just as it would be under the straight-line or units of production methods.

PROBLEM 1: On January 1, BlueCo, which uses 150% declining balance depreciation, acquires manufacturing equipment for which it shows the following data:

Cost	$80,000
Sales tax	$ 6,200
Delivery charge	$ 3,500
Installation and testing	$10,300
Estimated life	4 years
Residual value	$15,000

How is depreciation computed in each year of the equipment's 4-year life?

SOLUTION 1: To compute the acquisition cost:

$ 80,000	cost
6,200	sales tax
3,500	delivery charge
10,300	installation and testing
$100,000	acquisition cost

To compute the depreciation rate:

$$\frac{1.00}{4 \text{ years (estimated life)}} = 25\% \times 150\% = 37.5\% \text{ depreciation rate}$$

The computation for each year's depreciation is shown in the following table:

Year ending	Book value at beginning of year	Depreciation expense for the year	Credit to Accum. Depr.	Year-end balance in Accum. Depr.	Year-end book value
12/31/X1	$100,000	$100,000 x 37.5% = $37,500	$37,500	$37,500	$62,500
12/31/X2	62,500	$ 62,500 x 37.5% = 23,438*	23,438	60,938	39,062
12/31/X3	39,062	$ 39,062 x 37.5% = 14,648*	14,648	75,586	24,414
12/31/X4	24,414	9,414**	9,414	85,000	15,000

*Rounded
**Plug number

How the plug number was computed: Because the residual value is $15,000, depreciation taken in the last year is $9,414. The $9,414 for the last year is greater than the computed amount of $9,155 ($24,414 year beginning book value x 37.5% = $9,155 [rounded]). Under the declining balance method, there is often some depreciation still to be taken after the last year. This leftover amount can be included with the final year's depreciation unless the company decides to revise the asset's estimated life.

Because this machine is used in manufacturing, depreciation is recorded to Inventory—Work-In-Process OH[1] (overhead), *not* Depreciation Expense, as follows:

For Year 1

Inventory—Work-In-Process OH	37,500	
Accumulated Depreciation—Equipment		37,500

---

1. To see why the account Inventory—Work-In-Process OH is used, see the note on page 19.

<u>For Year 2</u>

Inventory—Work-In-Process OH	23,438	
Accumulated Depreciation—Equipment		23,438

<u>For Year 3</u>

Inventory—Work-In-Process OH	14,648	
Accumulated Depreciation—Equipment		14,648

And so on.

PROBLEM 2: On January 1, BarCo, which uses double-declining balance depreciation, acquires equipment that has an original cost of $100,000, an estimated life of 10 years and an estimated residual value of $10,000. What is the annual depreciation in each of the 10 years?

SOLUTION 2: First, <u>compute the depreciation rate</u>:

$$\frac{1.00}{10 \text{ years (estimated life)}} = 0.1 \times 200\% = 20\% \text{ depreciation rate}$$

<u>To compute the annual depreciation for Year 1</u>:
$100,000 beginning book value x 20% = $20,000 depreciation

At the end of Year 1, the book value is $80,000 ($100,000 original cost – $20,000 accumulated depreciation). The Year 1 ending book value becomes the Year 2 beginning book value.

<u>To compute depreciation for Year 2</u>:
$80,000 beginning book value x 20% depreciation rate = $16,000 depreciation for Year 2

The depreciation amounts and computations for Years 1–10 are shown in the table on the next page:

Year ending	Book value at beginning of year	Depreciation expense for the year		Credit to Accum. Depr.	Year-end balance in Accum. Depr.	Year-end book value
12/31/X1	$100,000	$100,000 x 20% =	$20,000	$20,000	$20,000	$80,000
12/31/X2	80,000	$ 80,000 x 20% =	16,000	16,000	36,000	64,000
12/31/X3	64,000	$ 64,000 x 20% =	12,800	12,800	48,800	51,200
12/31/X4	51,200	$ 51,200 x 20% =	10,240	10,240	59,040	40,960
12/31/X5	40,960	$ 40,960 x 20% =	8,192	8,192	67,232	32,768
12/31/X6	32,768	$ 32,768 x 20% =	6,554	6,554	73,786	26,214
12/31/X7	26,214	$ 26,214 x 20% =	5,243	5,243	79,029	20,971
12/31/X8	20,971	$ 20,971 x 20% =	4,194	4,194	83,223	16,777
12/31/X9	16,777	$ 16,777 x 20% =	3,355	3,355	86,578	13,422
12/31/X10	13,422		3,422*	3,422*	90,000	10,000

*Plug number

How the plug number was computed: Because the residual value is $10,000, depreciation taken in the last year is $3,422. The $3,422 for the last year is greater than the computed amount of $2,684 ($13,422 year beginning book value x 20% = $2,684 [rounded]). Under the declining balance method, there is often some depreciation still to be taken after the last year. This leftover amount can be included with the final year's depreciation unless the company decides to revise the asset's estimated life.

After depreciation of $3,422 is taken in Year 10, the book value will equal the residual value of $10,000, and the total balance in Accumulated Depreciation will equal the depreciable base of $90,000.

When Assets Are Acquired During the Year

To depreciate assets acquired during the year, multiply the portion of the year for which depreciation is taken by the annual depreciation amount as you would if you were using the straight-line method. But, under the declining balance method, unlike the straight-line method, depreciation not taken in the first year is not taken in the final year. Instead, the company continues to compute depreciation in subsequent years based on the declining balance, regardless of whether depreciation taken in the first year was for part or all of the year.

PROBLEM 3: On June 1, MiCo acquires equipment with an original cost of $75,000, an estimated life of 5 years and a residual value of $5,000. MiCo uses double-declining balance of depreciation. What is MiCo's depreciation for Years 1–5?

SOLUTION 3: First, compute the depreciation rate:

$$\frac{1.00}{5 \text{ years (estimated life)}} = 0.2 \times 200\% = 40\% \text{ depreciation rate}$$

To compute depreciation for the *entire* first year:
$75,000 book value (same as acquisition cost in the first year) x 40% depreciation rate = $30,000 depreciation for the entire first year

To compute depreciation for the portion of Year 1 when the machine was in use:
$30,000 depreciation for the first year x $\frac{7}{12}$ (7 months, June–December that the equipment was used) = $17,500 depreciation for Year 1

To compute depreciation for Year 2:
$75,000 original cost – $17,500 first-year depreciation = $57,500 Year 1 ending book value, which becomes Year 2 beginning book value x 40% depreciation rate = $23,000 depreciation for Year 2

Depreciation for Years 1–5 is shown in the following table:

Year ending	Book value at beginning of year	Depreciation expense for the year		Credit to Accum. Depr.	Year-end balance in Accum. Depr.	Year-end book value
12/31/X1	$75,000	$75,000 x 40% x 7/12 =	$17,500	$17,500	$17,500	$57,500
12/31/X2	57,500	$57,500 x 40% =	23,000	23,000	40,500	34,500
12/31/X3	34,500	$34,500 x 40% =	13,800	13,800	54,300	20,700
12/31/X4	20,700	$20,700 x 40% =	8,280	8,280	62,580	12,420
12/31/X5	12,420	$12,420 x 40% =	4,968	4,968	67,548	7,452
12/31/X6	7,452		2,452*	2,452*	70,000	5,000

*Plug number.

How the plug number was computed: Although computed depreciation in the last year is $2,981 (rounded) ($7,452 book value x 40%), only $2452 can be taken if the asset is not to be depreciated beyond its residual value. To compute: $7,452 beginning 20X6 book value – $5,000 residual value = $2,452 maximum depreciation to be taken in 20X6.

Completing the Depreciation Schedule at Year End

The example of PlatCo, a manufacturer of dishware that prepares its financial statements under GAAP, is continued here from Sections 3 and 4. There is no need to look back; the relevant information is provided here.

During 2008, PlatCo does the following:

- On March 1, PlatCo acquires for $75,000 a minicomputer with special software to design new product lines. The system, which will be used only for manufacturing, has an estimated life of 4 years and a residual value of $30,000 and will be depreciated under the declining balance method at an annual depreciation rate of 150%.

- On March 30, PlatCo purchases a used packaging machine for $115,000, a real bargain. But the reason the equipment is so cheap is that within 3 years new equipment will be coming out that produces and packages in one operation the kind of product that PlatCo sells. Therefore, PlatCo estimates that the equipment will have a 3-year life, optimistically estimates a residual value of $10,000 and decides to depreciate the equipment under the DDB method.

- On April 30, it sells the Dodge van because it had to have three or four repairs in the first 2 months of use. During 2008, the van was used to deliver only 632 cartons. Until business picks up, PlatCo will not replace it. (See the schedule on page 98 for the depreciation rate).

- During 2008, the water purifier is used to purify 198,000 gallons. (See schedule on page 98 for rate.)

- During 2008 the plastic extruder is used to produce 138,000 tops. (See schedule on page 98 for rate.)

On page 98 is a photocopy of PlatCo's depreciation schedule, which is complete through 2007. Complete the 2008 depreciation and accumulated depreciation for all of PlatCo's current and new assets using the appropriate depreciation method. Then total the 2008 depreciation and accumulated depreciation columns and record the 2008 year-end adjusting entries. Check your work against the completed 2008 columns on page 99 and against the year-end journal entries on page 102.

Before you can complete the schedule for 2008, you need to compute depreciation expense for the various assets. Try to do these computations before looking at how they are done below.

To compute 2008 depreciation for the minicomputer system:
$1.00 \div 4$-year estimated life = 25% straight-line rate x 150% = 37.5% declining balance rate x \$75,000 book value (same as acquisition cost in the first year) = \$28,125 x $^{10}\!/_{12}$ of the year (March–December) = \$23,438 (rounded) depreciation in 2008.

To compute 2008 depreciation for the packaging machine:
$1.00 \div 3$-year estimated life = 33.3% straight-line rate x 200% = 66.6% declining balance rate x \$115,000 book value (same as acquisition cost in the first year) =\$76,590 x $^{9}\!/_{12}$ of the year (March–December) = \$57,443 depreciation for 2008.

To compute 2008 depreciation for the Dodge van:
632 cartons hauled in 2008 x \$.80 (per carton) depreciation rate = \$506 (rounded) depreciation expense for 2008.

To compute 2008 depreciation for the water purifier:
198,000 gallons x \$.05 (per gallon) = \$9,900 depreciation expense for 2008.

To compute 2008 depreciation for the plastic extruder:
138,000 tops produced x \$.09 (per plastic top) depreciation rate = \$12,420 depreciation expense for 2008.

Depreciation Schedule (2007)

Methods
SL = straight-line
DB = declining balance
SYD = sum-of-the-years'-digits

KIND OF PROPERTY	DATE ACQUIRED	METHOD	RATE OR LIFE	DEPRECIABLE COST OR OTHER BASIS	RESIDUAL (SALVAGE) VALUE	DEPRECIATION IN PRIOR YEARS	DEPRECIATION FOR YR. ENDED 12/31/07	ACCUMULATED DEPRECIATION 12/31/07	DEPRECIATION FOR YR. ENDED	ACCUMULATED DEPRECIATION	DEPRECIATION FOR YR. ENDED	ACCUMULATED DEPRECIATION
Property												
Office Building	1/5/00	SL	30 yrs	300,000	100,000	70,000	10,000	80,000				
Land for ofc. bldg.	1/5/00	NA		55,000								
Warehouse	11/12/72	SL	4%	90,000	25,000	90,000		90,000				
Land for warehouse	11/12/72	NA		32,000								
Equipment												
Boiler (80% man.)	1/1/01	SL	15 yrs	75,000	10,000	30,000	5,000	35,000				
Air filter (100% man.)	7/2/03	SL	8 yrs	88,000	5,000	38,500	11,000	49,500				
Water pur. (70% man.)	2/17/07	UOP	$.05/gal.	65,000	15,000		7,500	7,500				
Extruder (100% man.)	12/20/07	UOP	$.09/unit	90,000	30,000		900	900				
Vehicles												
Oldsmobile	11/3/04	SL	6 yrs	18,000	6,000	6,500	3,000	9,500				
Delivery van (used)	1/14/05	SL	20%	20,000	5,000	8,000	4,000	12,000				
Dodge van (used)	6/30/07	UOP	$.80/ctn.	8,000	7,000		1,840	1,840				
Totals				841,000	203,000	243,000	43,240	286,240				

Depreciation Schedule (2008)

Methods
SL = straight-line
DB = declining balance
SD = sum-of-the-years'-digits

KIND OF PROPERTY	DATE ACQUIRED	METHOD	RATE OR LIFE	DEPRECIABLE COST OR OTHER BASIS	RESIDUAL (SALVAGE) VALUE	DEPRECIATION IN PRIOR YEARS	DEPRECIATION FOR YR. ENDED 12/31/07	ACCUMULATED DEPRECIATION 12/31/07	DEPRECIATION FOR YR. ENDED 12/31/08	ACCUMULATED DEPRECIATION 12/31/08	DEPRECIATION FOR YR. ENDED	ACCUMULATED DEPRECIATION
Property												
Office Building	1/5/00	SL	30 yrs	300,000	100,000	70,000	10,000	80,000	10,000	90,000		
Land for ofc. bldg.	1/5/00	NA		55,000								
Warehouse	11/12/72	SL	4%	90,000	25,000	90,000		90,000		90,000		
Land for warehouse	11/12/72	NA		32,000								
Equipment												
Boiler (80% man.)	1/1/01	SL	15 yrs	75,000	10,000	30,000	5,000	35,000	5,000	40,000		
Air filter (100% man.)	7/2/03	SL	8 yrs	88,000	5,000	38,500	11,000	49,500	11,000	60,500		
Water pur. (70% man.)	2/17/07	UOP	$.05/gal.	65,000	15,000		7,500	7,500	9,900	17,400		
Extruder (100% man.)	12/20/07	UOP	$.09/unit	90,000	30,000		900	900	12,420	13,320		
Minicom. (100% man.)	3/1/08	**150DB**	**37.5%**	**45,000**	**30,000**				23,438	23,438		
Pack. mach. (100% man.)	3/30/08	**DDB**	**66.6%**	**105,000**	**10,000**				57,443	57,443		
Vehicles												
Oldsmobile	11/3/04	SL	6 yrs	18,000	6,000	6,500	3,000	9,500	3,000	12,500		
Delivery van (used)	1/14/05	SL	20%	20,000	5,000	8,000	4,000	12,000	4,000	16,000		
Dodge van (used)	6/30/07	UOP	$.80/ctn.	8,000	7,000		1,840	1,840	506	SOLD		
Totals				991,000	243,000	243,000	43,240	286,240	136,707	420,601		

Notes on the depreciation schedule:

- The newly acquired assets, minicomputer and packaging machine, are in boldface type.

- 2008 depreciation expense and accumulated depreciation are in boldface type.

- Land included in the purchase of the office building and warehouse is presented on the schedule even though it is not depreciated because most firms show *all* assets on their depreciation schedules.

- Assets used partly or entirely for manufacturing show the percentage of use allocated to manufacturing next to them so that anyone who reads the schedule will be able to make the year-end adjusting entries correctly. This is one of many ways to show the allocation.

- Although the warehouse was fully depreciated years ago, PlatCo continues to present this and every other asset the company owns on the depreciation schedule until the asset is disposed of.

- Depreciation is shown for the Dodge van that was sold during the year, but accumulated depreciation is not. That is because when the van was sold on April 30, the accumulated depreciation for this asset would have been removed from the books at the same time. (Disposal of plant and equipment assets is not covered in this course.)

- Even though computation of depreciation under the declining balance method uses the asset's book value rather than its depreciable base, the schedule still shows the minicomputer's and packaging machine's depreciable base and residual value simply because that is how the schedule happened to be designed. Each asset's acquisition cost is the total of these two items (depreciable base + residual value).

In calculating depreciation for PlatCo, you would take the following steps to make sure that all PlatCo's assets had been depreciated in 2008:

1. Total the depreciable cost column, then total the residual value column. Add the totals from the two columns to yield the total acquisition cost of all assets that PlatCo is depreciating in 2008. To compute:

$ 991,000	total "depreciable cost or other basis" of all assets on the depreciation schedule
243,000	total residual value of all assets on the depreciation schedule
$1,234,000	total acquisition cost of all assets on the depreciation schedule

2. Subtract the acquisition cost of any assets on the 2008 schedule that were sold during 2008.

$1,234,000	total acquisition cost of all assets on the depreciation schedule
– 15,000	acquisition cost of Dodge van
$1,219,000	total acquisition cost of all assets owned by the company at year-end 2008

3. To verify the depreciation schedule, go to the general ledger and total all plant and equipment asset account balances (each balance represents an asset's acquisition cost). The total should be $1,219,000. If the total of all depreciable asset account balances is more than $1,219,000, then somewhere there is another asset that PlatCo has omitted. If the total is less than $1,219,000, then the schedule may list an asset that the company no longer owns, or there is an error.

By including land on the depreciation schedule, you can quickly check the schedule against the general ledger asset accounts. If land had been left off the schedule, you would have to add the balances of only the *depreciable* accounts, increasing the likelihood of errors and undermining the crosscheck.

Two adjusting entries are required to record PlatCo's depreciation expense for 2008. The first entry allocates depreciation for nonmanufacturing assets to the Depreciation Expense account. This entry will include depreciation for most of the depreciable assets.

The data that you need to allocate depreciation for the minicomputer, packaging machine, extruder and Dodge van were given on page 97.

The data that you need to allocate depreciation for the air filter and boiler were given in Section 3 and are repeated here. The air filter is used 100% by the factory. The boiler is used 80% by the factory (manufacturing) and 20% by the offices.

The first entry records depreciation to Depreciation Expense:

Depreciation Expense	21,476*	
Accumulated Depreciation—Buildings		10,000
Accumulated Depreciation—Equipment		3,970**
Accumulated Depreciation—Vehicles		7,506

*$10,000	office building
1,000	boiler ($5,000 depreciation x 20% office use)
2,970	water purifier ($9,900 depreciation x 30% office use as noted on the schedule)
3,000	Oldsmobile
4,000	delivery van
506	Dodge van
$21,476	

**$1,000 boiler + $2,970 water purifier

The second entry allocates depreciation to the Inventory—Work-In-Process OH account:

Inventory—Work-In-Process OH	115,231*	
Accumulated Depreciation—Equipment		115,231

*$ 4,000	boiler ($5,000 depreciation x 80% used for manufacturing as noted on the schedule)
11,000	air filter
6,930	water purifier ($9,900 depreciation x 70% used for manufacturing as noted on the schedule)
12,420	plastic extruder (100% used for manufacturing as noted on the schedule)
23,438	minicomputer (100% used for manufacturing as noted on the schedule)
57,443	packaging machine (100% used for manufacturing as noted on the schedule)
$115,231	

The total depreciation expense in these two entries should equal total depreciation on the schedule. To compute:

$ 21,476	allocated to Depreciation Expense
115,231	allocated to Inventory—Work-In-Process OH
$136,707	total depreciation taken for 2008 on the schedule

If PlatCo decides to sell or trade-in a depreciable asset, you must bring the accumulated depreciation up to date as of the date of disposal. In Accumulated Depreciation, you will find total depreciation for *all* buildings, or *all* equipment or *all* vehicles, rather than for the particular asset that was disposed of. But on the depreciation schedule, you will find total depreciation for each asset as of the end of the prior year. Simply add accumulated depreciation taken in the current year to find total accumulated depreciation to date.

Revising the Estimated Life

It is not unusual for a company to discover that it has made an incorrect estimate of an asset's life or residual value. When this occurs, the company's CPA can revise the estimated life or the residual value and compute the new annual depreciation expense.

QUIZ 1   THE DECLINING BALANCE METHOD OF DEPRECIATION

NOTE: Where journal entries are required, it is sufficient to use the account title "Accumulated Depreciation." You are not required to add a description such as "Accumulated Depreciation—Equipment" because different companies use different descriptive words. If the answer uses the account Accumulated Depreciation—Equipment, but you used Accumulated Depreciation, take full credit.

Problem I.

Multiple choice. Circle the correct answer.

1. Under the declining balance method, annual depreciation equals the depreciation rate multiplied by . . .

   a. (cost – residual value).
   b. units produced.
   c. the book value.
   d. the depreciable base.

2. Under the straight-line method, total depreciation over the life of the asset equals the _____; under the declining balance method, total depreciation over the life of the asset equals the _____.

   a. depreciable base, book value
   b. book value, acquisition cost
   c. depreciable base, depreciable base
   d. book value, book value

3. The declining balance method provides _____ depreciation in the early years and _____ in the later years compared to straight-line depreciation.

   a. more, less
   b. less, more
   c. the same, the same

4. Under the double-declining balance method, the depreciation rate is calculated as . . .

a. $\dfrac{1.00}{\text{asset life}}$

b. $\dfrac{1.00}{\text{asset life}}$ x 200%

c. $\dfrac{1.00}{\text{acquisition cost}}$ x 200%

d. $\dfrac{1.00}{\text{residual value}}$ x 200%

Use the following information for Questions 5–8: PliCo acquires equipment with an original cost of $140,000 that the company expects to use for 8 years and to have a residual value of $5,000. PliCo uses the double- declining balance method.

5. The depreciation rate on the equipment is . . .

a. 25%   b. 15%   c. 10%   d. 5%

6. If the equipment is purchased at the beginning of 20X1, then 20X1 depreciation is . . .

a. $70,000   b. $60,000   c. $35,000   d. $30,000

7. If the equipment is purchased on September 1, 20X2, then first-year depreciation is . . .

a. $23,333   b. $20,000   c. $11,667   d. $10,000

8. The total depreciation that PliCo can take for the building over its useful life is . . .

a. $145,000   b. $140,000   c. $135,000   d. $5,000

Problem II.

You have the following data for equipment acquired by your company and depreciated under the double-declining balance method:

Invoice cost	$8,000
Sales tax	$ 800
Installation	$1,700
Useful life	3 years

The equipment will have no residual value at the end of its estimated life.

1. What is the depreciation rate for the equipment?

2. If the equipment were installed at the beginning of January, what is first-year depreciation?

3. If the equipment were installed on August 1, what is first-year depreciation?

4. If the equipment were installed on August 1, what is second-year depreciation?

Problem III.

On January 1, 20X1, your company acquires a computer that has an acquisition cost of $14,000, a residual value of $500 and a useful life of 4 years. Your company ends up using the asset for 5 years. Complete the following table using the double-declining balance method:

Year ending	Book value at beginning of year	Depreciation expense for the year	Credit to Accum. Depr.	Year-end balance in Accum. Depr.	Year-end book value
12/31/X1					
12/31/X2					
12/31/X3					
12/31/X4					

QUIZ 1   *Solutions and Explanations*

Problem I.

1. c

Under the declining balance method, the book value (not the depreciable base) is used to compute annual depreciation.

2. c

Even though the computation of depreciation under the declining balance method uses book value rather than depreciable base, the total depreciation permitted over the life of the asset is the same as under straight-line.

3. a

4. b

5. a

To compute the depreciation rate:

$$\frac{1.00}{8 \text{ years (estimated life)}} = 12.5\% \times 200\% = 25\% \text{ depreciation rate}$$

6. c

To compute:

$140,000 book value x 25% depreciation rate = $35,000 depreciation for 20X1

7. c

To compute:

$35,000 first-year depreciation (computed in Question 6) x $\frac{4}{12}$ (for the 4 months September – December) = $11,667 (rounded) depreciation

8. c

Total depreciation over the life of an asset is limited to its depreciable base. To compute:

$140,000 acquisition cost – $5,000 residual value = $135,000 depreciable base

Problem II.

1. 66.67%
To compute:

$$\frac{1.00}{3 \text{ years (estimated life)}} = \begin{array}{c} 33\% \times 200\% = 66.67\% \text{ (rounded)} \\ \text{depreciation rate} \end{array}$$

2. $7,000
To compute the acquisition cost:

$ 8,000	invoice cost
800	sales tax
1,700	installation
$10,500	acquisition cost

$10,500 book value (in the first year, the book value is the same as the acquisition cost) x 66.67% depreciation rate = $7,000 (rounded) first-year depreciation

3. $2,917
To compute:

$7,000 first year depreciation (computed in Question 2) x $\frac{5}{12}$ (for the 5 months August – December) = $2,917 (rounded) depreciation for the year

4. $5,056
To compute the book value at the beginning of the second year:

$10,500 acquisition cost – $2,917 Year 1 ending balance in accumulated depreciation (computed in Question 3) = $7,583 Year 1 ending book value, which is also Year 2 beginning book value

$7,583 Year 2 beginning book value x 66.67% depreciation rate = $5,056 (rounded) Year 2 depreciation

Problem III.

First, compute the depreciation rate:

$$\frac{1.00}{4 \text{ years (estimated life)}} = 25\% \times 200\% = 50\% \text{ depreciation rate}$$

The computation for each year's depreciation is shown in the table:

Year ending	Book value at beginning of year	Depreciation expense for the year	Credit to Accum. Depr.	Year-end balance in Accum. Depr.	Year-end book value
12/31/X1	$14,000	$14,000 x 50% = $7,000	$7,000	$ 7,000	$7,000
12/31/X2	7,000	$ 7,000 x 50% = 3,500	3,500	10,500	3,500
12/31/X3	3,500	$ 3,500 x 50% = 1,750	1,750	12,250	1,750
12/31/X4	1,750	$1,250	1,250	13,500	500

*Depreciation in the fourth year is a plug number, $1,250. This is the maximum depreciation that can be taken so that total accumulated depreciation does not exceed the residual value of $500. After the $1,250 is taken, total accumulated depreciation equals the depreciable cost of $13,500 and the book value equals the residual value of $500.

If the company uses the computer for a 5th year, no depreciation is taken in that year because the computer is fully depreciated.

QUIZ 2   THE DECLINING BALANCE METHOD OF DEPRECIATION

Problem I.

Mark each statement True or False.

1. The declining balance method results in an equal amount of depreciation in each year.

    a. True   b. False

2. Residual value represents an estimate of the asset's value at the end of its useful life.

    a. True   b. False

3. Under the declining balance method, the book value at the end of each year is the residual value.

    a. True   b. False

4. When an asset being depreciated under the declining balance method is used only 4 months in the first year, depreciation does not have to be prorated.

    a. True   b. False

5. Under the declining balance method, annual depreciation = depreciation rate x book value.

    a. True   b. False

Problem II.

Equipment acquired on January 1, 20X1, for $23,000 has a residual value of $2,000 and an estimated life of 4 years. Use the double-declining balance method to compute the depreciation for . . .

1. 20X1.

2. 20X2.

3. 20X3.

4. 20X4.

Problem III.

An asset with an original cost of $35,000, a residual value of $1,500 and an expected life of 10 years is acquired on January 1, 20X1. The company uses the double-declining balance method. Complete the following table:

Year ending	Book value at beginning of year	Depreciation expense for the year	Credit to Accum. Depr.	Year-end balance in Accum. Depr.	Year-end book value
12/31/X1					
12/31/X2					
12/31/X3					
12/31/X4					

Problem IV.

You are given the following data for a computer purchase:

Invoice cost	$5,400
Sales tax	$ 500
Delivery charges	$ 200
Installation and programming	$ 900
Expected residual value	$2,000
Expected useful life	5 years
Date of acquisition	August 1, 20X1

Under double-declining balance depreciation, show the depreciation for . . .

1. 20X1.

2. 20X2.

QUIZ 2 *Solutions and Explanations*

1. False
   The declining balance method results in more depreciation in the early years, less in the later years.

2. True
   Residual value is an estimate of what can be recovered for the asset when it is disposed of (sold or traded in) at the end of its useful life.

3. False
   Under all GAAP depreciation methods, residual value is the book value at the end of the asset's life when all depreciation has been taken.

4. False
   Annual depreciation is prorated for the first year based on when the asset was put into use.

5. True

Problem II.

1. $11,500 depreciation
   To compute:

   $$\frac{1.00}{4 \text{ years (estimated life)}} = 25\% \times 200\% = 50\% \text{ depreciation rate}$$

   $23,000 book value x 50% = $11,500 depreciation for 20X1

2. $5,750
   The ending book value for 20X1 was $11,500 ($23,000 acquisition cost – $11,500 balance in accumulated depreciation = $11,500 ending book value for 20X1 and beginning book value for 20X2)

   $11,500 year-beginning 20X2 book value x 50% = $5,750 depreciation for 20X2

3. $2,875

The ending book value for 20X2 was $5,750 ($23,000 acquisition cost – $17,250* balance in accumulated depreciation = $5,750 ending book value for 20X2 and beginning book value for 20X3)

*$11,500 depreciation from 20X1 + $5,750 depreciation from 20X2

$5,750 beginning 20X3 book value x 50% depreciation rate = $2,875 depreciation for 20X3

4. $875

Careful analysis reveals that you will have to use a plug number for 20X4:

$11,500	accumulated depreciation for 20X1
5,750	accumulated depreciation for 20X2
– 2,875	accumulated depreciation for 20X3
$20,125	balance in Accumulated Depreciation at the beginning of 20X4

$21,000	depreciable base ($23,000 acquisition cost – $2,000 residual value)
–20,125	balance in Accumulated Depreciation at the beginning of 20X4
$ 875	maximum depreciation allowed in 20X4

The computed depreciation cannot bring the book value below the residual value. To compute:

The ending book value for 20X3 was $2,875 ($23,000 acquisition cost – $20,125 balance in accumulated depreciation), and this is the beginning book value for 20X4. $2,875 beginning 20X4 book value x 50% = $1,438 (rounded) depreciation for 20X4, which is much greater than the maximum of $875 permitted.

Problem III.

To compute the depreciation rate:

$$\frac{1.00}{10 \text{ years (estimated life)}} = 10\% \times 200\% = 20\% \text{ depreciation rate}$$

The computation for each year's depreciation is shown on the following table:

Year ending	Book value at beginning of year	Depreciation expense for the year	Credit to Accum. Depr.	Year-end balance in Accum. Depr.	Year-end book value
12/31/X1	$35,000	$35,000 x 20% = $7,000	$7,000	$ 7,000	$28,000
12/31/X2	28,000	$28,000 x 20% = 5,600	5,600	12,600	22,400
12/31/X3	22,400	$22,400 x 20% = 4,480	4,480	17,080	17,920
12/31/X4	17,920	$17,920 x 20% = 3,584	3,584	20,664	14,336

Problem IV.

First compute the acquisition cost:

$5,400	invoice cost
500	sales tax
200	delivery
900	installation and programming
$7,000	total cost of the computer

Then compute the depreciation rate:

$$\frac{1.00}{5 \text{ years (estimated life)}} = 20\% \times 200\% = 40\% \text{ depreciation rate}$$

1. Depreciation for 20X1 is $1,167
To compute:

$7,000 book value (same as acquisition cost in first year) x 40% depreciation rate = $2,800 x $\frac{5}{12}$ (for the 5 months August – December) = $1,167 (rounded)

2. Depreciation for 20X2 is $2,333
To compute:

$7,000 acquisition cost – $1,167 accumulated depreciation at the end of 20X1 = $5,833, which is the ending book value for 20X1 and the beginning book value for 20X2 x 40% depreciation rate = $2,333 (rounded) depreciation for 20X2

Section 6

THE SUM-OF-THE-YEARS'-DIGITS METHOD OF DEPRECIATION

Introduction

The sum-of-the years'-digits (SYD) method, like the declining balance (DB) method, results in more depreciation in the early years of an asset's life and less in later years. But under SYD depreciation the year-to-year decline in depreciation expense is more gradual than under DB depreciation. Today, SYD is the least-used of the four GAAP methods.

Computing Depreciation Under the SYD Method

To compute depreciation under the SYD method, multiply the depreciable base by the depreciation rate. Under SYD, the depreciation rate is a fraction that is used as follows:

$$\frac{\textbf{Numerator}}{\textbf{Denominator}} = \frac{\text{Years remaining in asset's life}}{\text{SYD}} = \text{depreciation rate}$$

Depreciation rate x depreciable base = depreciation expense

The numerator: **Years remaining in the assets life as of the *beginning* of the year.** For example, if you are depreciating an asset with a 10-year estimated life, the numerator to use at the end of Year 1 is 10 because that is the number of years remaining in the asset's life as of the *beginning* of the first year. The numerator to use at the end of Year 2 is 9, because that is the number of years remaining in the asset's life as of the *beginning* of Year 2. Because the numerator changes each year, the SYD depreciation rate also changes each year.

The denominator: **sum-of-the-years' digits.** This is the total (sum) of the *digits* in the asset's life. For example, if there are 5 years in the asset's life, the sum of the digits is 15 (5 + 4 + 3 + 2 +1). If there are 3 years in the asset's life, the sum of the digits is 6 (3 + 2 + 1). The denominator stays the same each year. To save time in adding up the digits for each asset each year, use the following shortcut to compute the denominator:

$$\frac{n(n+1)}{2} = \text{SYD, the denominator in the fraction}$$

n = asset's estimated life

PROBLEM 1: On January 1, BryCo, which uses SYD depreciation, acquires[1] an asset with an estimated life of 10 years. What is the depreciation rate for Years 1–5?

SOLUTION 1: First, compute the denominator (sum-of-the-years'-digits) which will be used each year:

$$\frac{n(n+1)}{2} = \text{SYD}$$

n (estimated life) = 10

$$\frac{10 \times (10+1)}{2} = 55^* \text{ sum-of-the-years'-digits for a 10-year estimated life}$$

*10 + 9 + 8 + 7 + 6 + 5 + 4 + 3 + 2 + 1 = 55

The annual depreciation rates for the asset are as follows:

Year	Depreciation rate
Year 1	10/55
Year 2	9/55
Year 3	8/55
Year 4	7/55
Year 5	6/55

To compute annual depreciation expense each year, multiply that year's depreciation rate by the depreciable base.

---

1. Under both generally accepted accounting principles (GAAP) and tax law, depreciation cannot begin until the asset has been acquired *and* placed in service. However, to avoid cumbersome, repetitious language ("acquires and places in service . . ."), it is assumed throughout this course that the acquired asset is placed in service on the date of purchase.

PROBLEM 2: On January 1, 20X1, WyCo, which uses SYD depreciation, acquires a machine that has an estimated life of 5 years and a residual value of $10,000. WyCo pays the following invoice:

Machine	$90,000
Sales tax	$ 7,000
Installation	$ 3,000

What is the depreciation for each year?

SOLUTION 2: First, determine the depreciable base:

$ 90,000	machine
7,000	sales tax
3,000	installation
$100,000	depreciable base
− 10,000	residual value
$ 90,000	depreciable base

Next, compute the denominator that will be used in each year's depreciation rate:

$$\frac{n(n + 1)}{2} \quad \text{or} \quad \frac{5(5+1)}{2} \quad \text{or} \quad \frac{30}{2} \quad = \quad 15$$

The denominator (sum-of-the-year's-digits) for each year's depreciation rate is 15.

To compute depreciation for 20X1:

$90,000 depreciable base x $^{5*}/_{15}$ = $30,000 depreciation

*The numerator is the number of years remaining in the asset's life at the beginning of the year. Before the adjusting entry is recorded at the end of 20X1, all 5 years remain in the asset's life, so the numerator is 5.

To compute depreciation for 20X2:

$$\frac{4*}{15**} \quad x \quad \$90,000 = \$24,000 \text{ depreciation for 20X2}$$

*At the beginning of the second year, 4 years remain in the machine's life.

**$\frac{5(5+1)}{2}$

Depreciation in each year of the machine's life is shown in the following table:

Year ending	Depreciation expense for the year	Credit to Accum. Depreciation	Year-end balance in Accum. Depreciation	Year-end book value
01/01/X1				$100,000*
12/31/X1	5/15 x $90,000 = $30,000	$30,000	$30,000	70,000
12/31/X2	4/15 x $90,000 = 24,000	24,000	54,000	46,000
12/31/X3	3/15 x $90,000 = 18,000	18,000	72,000	28,000
12/31/X4	2/15 x $90,000 = 12,000	12,000	84,000	16,000
12/31/X5	1/15 x $90,000 = 6,000	6,000	90,000	10,000

*This is the original acquisition cost.

At the end of the machine's useful life, the balance in Accumulated Depreciation equals the depreciable base of $90,000, and the book value equals the residual value of $10,000—exactly the same amounts as if the machine were depreciated under the straight-line (SL), units of production (UOP) or declining balance (DB) methods.

PROBLEM 3: On January 1, 20X3, ProCo acquires and installs in its building an air-filtering system with an estimated life of 6 years and a residual value of $2,000. It pays the following invoice:

Machine	$20,000
Sales tax	$1,500
Freight	$2,500

ProCo determines that 75% of the building is used for manufacturing and 25% for office space. Show the computation for all 5 years and the adjusting entries for depreciation at the end of the first 2 years.

SOLUTION 3: First compute the depreciable base:

$20,000	machine
1,500	sales tax
2,500	freight
$24,000	acquisition cost
– 2,000	residual value
$22,000	depreciable base

Next, compute the denominator that will be used in each year's depreciation rate:

$$\frac{n(n + 1)}{2} \quad \text{or} \quad \frac{6(6+1)}{2} = 21, \text{ the denominator of the fraction of each year's depreciation rate}$$

To compute depreciation for 20X3:

$$\frac{6 \text{ years remaining in the machine's life}}{21} \times \$22,000 = \$6,286 \text{ (rounded) depreciation for 20X3}$$

To record 20X3 depreciation allocated to office use:

Depreciation Expense	1,571	
Accumulated Depreciation—Equipment		1,571

$6,286 depreciation for 20X3 x 25% office use = $1,571 (rounded)

To record 20X3 depreciation allocated to manufacturing:

Inventory—Work-In-Process OH*[1]	4,715	
Accumulated Depreciation—Equipment		4,715

*Overhead

$6,286 depreciation for 20X3 x 75% used for manufacturing = $4,715 (rounded)

To compute depreciation for 20X4:

$$\frac{5 \text{ years remaining in the machine's life}}{21} \times \$22,000 = \$5,238 \text{ (rounded) depreciation for 20X4}$$

To record 20X4 depreciation allocated to the office:

Depreciation Expense	1,309	
Accumulated Depreciation—Equipment		1,309

$5,238 depreciation for 20X4 x 25% office use = $1,309 (rounded)

---

1. For an explanation of why the account Inventory—Work-In-Process OH is used, see the note on page 19.

To record 20X4 depreciation allocated to manufacturing:

Inventory—Work-In-Process OH   3,929
    Accumulated Depreciation—Equipment   3,929

$5,238 depreciation for 20X4 x 75% used for manufacturing = $3,929 (rounded)

The computations for depreciation are as follows:

Year ending	Depreciation expense for the year	Credit to Accum. Depreciation	Year-end balance in Accum. Depreciation	Year-end book value
01/01/X3				$24,000*
12/31/ X3	6/21 x $22,000 = $6,286	$6,286	$ 6,286	17,714
12/31/ X4	5/21 x $22,000 = 5,238	5,238	11,524	12,476
12/31/ X5	4/21 x $22,000 = 4,190	4,190	15,714	8,286
12/31/ X6	3/21 x $22,000 = 3,143	3,143	18,857	5,143
12/31/ X7	2/21 x $22,000 = 2,095	2,095	20,952	3,048
12/31/ X8	1/21 x $22,000 = 1,048	1,048	22,000	2,000

* This is the acquisition cost.

In each year from 20X5 to 20X9, the company will allocate 25% of the depreciation to Depreciation Expense and 75% of the depreciation to Inventory—Work-In-Process OH. Both entries will credit Accumulated Depreciation—Equipment.

When Assets Are Acquired During the Year

When assets are acquired during the year, such as on June 1, the SYD method requires the company to take a full 12 months of depreciation at the same depreciation rate. For example, if your company buys an asset on August 1, 20X0 and the first-year depreciation rate is, say, 5/15, then your company must use the 5/15 depreciation rate through July 31, 20X1. This is different from the straight-line and declining balance methods, which break off first-year depreciation on December 31 (or other fiscal year end) and use up the remaining depreciation in the last year of the asset's life.

PROBLEM 4: On June 1, 20X1, StraCo acquires a machine that has an acquisition cost of $50,000, an estimated life of 4 years and a residual value of $500. What is the depreciation for each year?

SOLUTION 4: First, find the depreciable base: $50,000 original cost – $500 residual value = $49,500 depreciable base.

Next, compute the denominator that will be used in each year's depreciation rate:

$$\frac{n(n + 1)}{2} \quad \text{or} \quad \frac{4(4+1)}{2} = 10, \text{ the denominator of each year's depreciation rate}$$

Compute depreciation for the first 12 months:

$$\frac{4 \text{ years remaining in the machine's life}}{10} \times \$49,500 = \$19,800 \text{ depreciation for the first 12 months}$$

Of the $19,800 depreciation taken for the first 12 months, 7 months' depreciation is allocated to the first calendar year, 20X1, and 5 months' depreciation is allocated to the second calendar year, 20X2.

To compute depreciation for 20X1:

$19,800 x $\frac{7}{12}$ = $11,550 depreciation for the 7 months, June-December, 20X1

To compute depreciation for 20X2:

For January-May, 20X2: $49,500 x $\frac{4}{10}$ = $19,800 x $\frac{5}{12}$ = $8,250 depreciation

For June-December, 20X2: $49,500 x $\frac{3}{10}$ = $14,850 x $\frac{7}{12}$ = $8,663 (rounded).

For the calendar year 20X2, total depreciation is $16,913 ($8,250 + $8,663).

Note that because the same SYD depreciation rate is used for 12 months, the same rate is applied to part of 20X1 and part of 20X2.

Beginning on June 1, 20X2, a new depreciation rate ($\frac{3}{10}$) is used for the next 12 months:

$$\frac{3 \text{ years remaining in the machine's life}}{10} \times \$49,500 = \$14,850 \text{ depreciation for the second 12 months}$$

To compute:

$14,850 x $\frac{7}{12}$ = $8,663 depreciation for 7 months (June-December, 20X2)
$14,850 x $\frac{5}{12}$ = $6,187 depreciation for 5 months (January-May, 20X3)

The following table shows depreciation for each year of the asset's life. Note that two columns are required to show annual depreciation. One column shows depreciation for 12 consecutive months using a single depreciation rate, and the column next to it shows depreciation for the calendar year, which includes two different depreciation rates: one rate for the first 7 months' depreciation, another for the last 5 months of the calendar year.

Year ending	12 months' depreciation rate and amount	Depreciation expense for the year		Credit to Accum. Depr.	Year balance in Accum. Depr.	Year-end book value
06/01/X1						$50,000*
12/31/X1	4/10 x $49,500 = $19,800	$19,800 x 7/12 = $11,550		$11,550	$11,550	38,450
12/31/X2	3/10 x $49,500 = 14,850	20X1: $19,800 x 5/12 = 20X2: $14,850 x 7/12 =	8,250 8,663 16,913	16,913	28,463	21,537
12/31/X3	2/10 x $49,500 = 9,900	20X2: $14,850 x 5/12 = 20X3: $ 9,900 x 7/12 =	6,187 5,775 11,962	11,962	40,425	9,575
12/31/X4	1/10 x 49,500 = 4,950	20X3: $ 9,900 x 5/12 = 20X4: $ 4,950 x 7/12 =	4,125 2,888 7,013	7,013	47,438	2,562
12/31/X5		20X4: 4,950 x 5/12 =	2,062	2,062	49,500	500

*This is the acquisition cost.

At the end of the asset's life, total accumulated depreciation ($49,500) equals the depreciable base, and book value at the end of the last year ($500) equals residual value, just as under SL, UOP and DB depreciation.

Comparing Depreciation Methods

The following table compares depreciation under the straight-line, double-declining balance and SYD methods on an asset purchased on January 1 with an original cost of $10,000, a residual value of $1,000 and a useful life of 5 years.

Year ending	Straight-line	Double-declining balance	Sum-of-the-years'-digits
12/31/X1	(9,000 x 20%) = $1,800	(10,000 x 40%) = $4,000	(5/15) x $9,000 = $3,000
12/31/X2	(9,000 x 20%) = 1,800	(6,000 x 40%) = 2,400	(4/15) x $9,000 = 2,400
12/31/X3	(9,000 x 20%) = 1,800	(3,600 x 40%) = 1,440	(3/15) x $9,000 = 1,800
12/31/X4	(9,000 x 20%) = 1,800	(2,160 x 40%) = 864	(2/15) x $9,000 = 1,200
12/31/X5	(9,000 x 20%) = 1,800	Plug number* 296	(1/15) x $9,000 = 600
Totals	$9,000	$9,000	$9,000

*The asset cannot exceed its depreciable base of $9,000 ($10,000 acquisition cost – $1,000 residual value). At 12/31/X5, total depreciation taken was $8,704 ($4,000 + $2,400 + $1,440 + $864). $9,000 depreciable base – $8,704 depreciation taken to date = $296 maximum depreciation allowable for the year ending 12/31/X5.

The asset's depreciable base for the straight-line and SYD methods is $9,000 ($10,000 original cost – $1,000 residual value).

Under all three methods, total depreciation over 5 years equals the depreciable base ($9,000). The declining balance method and the SYD method provide more depreciation in the early years, less in the later years. The straight-line method results in equal depreciation in each year. The units of production method (not shown) will vary depending upon output in each year, but total depreciation permitted will be the same as under the three methods shown.

Completing the Depreciation Schedule at Year End

The example of PlatCo, the manufacturer of dishware that prepares its financial statements under GAAP, is continued here from Sections 3, 4 and 5. There is no need to look back; everything is provided here.

During 2009, PlatCo does the following:

- On April 30, PlatCo acquires a new heating system for $115,000. It will be used 80% for manufacturing and 20% for the offices. The system, which has an estimated life of 15 years and a residual value of $20,000, will be depreciated under the SYD method.

- On December 5, PlatCo purchases a new air-conditioning system that, like the new heating system, will be used 80% for manufacturing and 20% for the offices. The new system cost $80,000, has an estimated life of 6 years, a residual value of $15,000, and will be depreciated under the SYD method.

- During 2009, the water purifier is used to purify 206,000 gallons. (See schedule on page 128 for rate.)

- During 2009, the plastic extruder is used to produce 168,000 tops. (See schedule on page 128 for rate.)

On page 128 is a photocopy of PlatCo's 2008 depreciation schedule, which is complete through 2008. Complete the 2009 depreciation and accumulated depreciation for all of PlatCo's current and new assets using the appropriate depreciation method and record the 2009 year-end adjusting entries. Compare your work against the completed 2009 columns on page 129 and the year-end journal entries on pages 132 and 133.

Before you can complete the schedule for 2009, you need to compute 2009 depreciation expense for the various assets. Try to do these computations before looking at how they are done below.

To compute 2009 depreciation for the heating system:

$115,000 acquisition cost − $20,000 residual value = $95,000 depreciable base. To compute the denominator that will be used in each year's depreciation rate: $\dfrac{n(n+1)}{2}$ or $\dfrac{15(15+1)}{2}$ or $\dfrac{240}{2}$ = 120 SYD denominator.

$95,000 depreciable base x $\dfrac{15\,{}^*}{120}$ = $11,875 depreciation for the next

12 months x $^8\!/_{12}$ (for the 8 months, May–December) = $7,917 (rounded) depreciation for 2009

*As of the beginning of the first year, all 15 years remain in the asset's life.

To compute 2009 depreciation for the A/C system:

$80,000 acquisition cost – $15,000 residual value = $65,000 depreciable base. To compute the denominator that will be used in each year's depreciation rate: $\dfrac{n(n+1)}{2}$ or $\dfrac{6(6+1)}{2}$ or $\dfrac{42}{2}$ = 21 SYD denominator.

$65,000 depreciable base x $\dfrac{6^*}{21}$ = $18,571 (rounded) depreciation for the next 12 months x $\frac{1}{12}$ (for December) = $1,548 (rounded) depreciation for 2009

*In the first year, all 6 years remain in the asset's life.

To compute 2009 depreciation for the water purifier:
206,000 gallons x $0.05 (per gallon) = $10,300 depreciation expense for 2009

To compute 2009 depreciation for the plastic extruder:

168,000 tops produced x $0.09 (per plastic top) depreciation rate = $15,120 depreciation expense for 2009

To compute 2009 depreciation for the minicomputer:

$75,000 book value in 2008 – $23,438 depreciation for 2008 (see schedule) = $51,562 beginning book value in 2009 x 37.5% (see schedule) declining balance rate = $19,336 (rounded) depreciation for 2009

To compute 2009 depreciation for the packaging machine:

$115,000 original cost – $57,443 first-year depreciation = $57,557 ending book value for 2008, which becomes 2009 beginning book value x 66.6% depreciation rate = $38,333 (rounded) depreciation for 2009

Depreciation Schedule (2008)

Methods
SL = straight line
DB = declining balance
SYD = sum-of-the-years'-digits

KIND OF PROPERTY	DATE ACQUIRED	METHOD	RATE OR LIFE	DEPRECIABLE COST OR OTHER BASIS	RESIDUAL (SALVAGE) VALUE	DEPRECIATION IN PRIOR YEARS	DEPRECIATION FOR YR. ENDED 12/31/07	ACCUMULATED DEPRECIATION 12/31/07	DEPRECIATION FOR YR. ENDED 12/31/08	ACCUMULATED DEPRECIATION 12/31/08	DEPRECIATION FOR YR. ENDED	ACCUMULATED DEPRECIATION
Property												
Office Building	1/5/00	SL	30 yrs	300,000	100,000	70,000	10,000	80,000	10,000	90,000		
Land for ofc. bldg.	1/5/00	NA		55,000								
Warehouse	11/12/72	SL	4%	90,000	25,000	90,000		90,000		90,000		
Land for warehouse	11/12/72	NA		32,000								
Equipment												
Boiler (80% man.)	1/1/01	SL	15 yrs	75,000	10,000	30,000	5,000	35,000	5,000	40,000		
Air filter (100% man.)	7/2/03	SL	8 yrs	88,000	5,000	38,500	11,000	49,500	11,000	60,500		
Water pur. (70% man.)	2/17/07	UOP	$.05/gal.	65,000	15,000		7,500	7,500	9,900	17,400		
Extruder (100% man.)	12/20/07	UOP	$.09/unit	90,000	30,000		900	900	12,420	13,320		
Minicom. (100% man.)	3/1/08	150DB	37.5%	45,000	30,000				23,438	23,438		
Pack. mach. (100% man.)	3/30/08	DDB	66.6%	105,000	10,000				57,443	57,443		
Vehicles												
Oldsmobile	11/3/04	SL	6 yrs	18,000	6,000	6,500	3,000	9,500	3,000	12,500		
Delivery van (used)	1/14/05	SL	20%	20,000	5,000	8,000	4,000	12,000	4,000	16,000		
Dodge van (used)	6/30/07	UOP	$.80/ctn.	8,000	7,000		1,840	1,840	506	SOLD		
Totals				991,000	243,000	243,000	43,240	286,240	136,707	420,601		

Depreciation Schedule (2009)

Methods
SL = straight line
DB = declining balance
SYD = sum-of-the-years'-digits

KIND OF PROPERTY	DATE ACQUIRED	METHOD	RATE OR LIFE	DEPRECIABLE COST OR OTHER BASIS	RESIDUAL (SALVAGE) VALUE	DEPRECIATION IN PRIOR YEARS	DEPRECIATION FOR YR. ENDED 12/31/07	ACCUMULATED DEPRECIATION 12/31/07	DEPRECIATION FOR YR. ENDED 12/31/08	ACCUMULATED DEPRECIATION 12/31/08	DEPRECIATION FOR YR. ENDED 12/31/09	ACCUMULATED DEPRECIATION 12/31/09
Property												
Office Building	1/5/00	SL	30 yrs	300,000	100,000	70,000	10,000	80,000	10,000	90,000	10,000	100,000
Land for ofc. bldg.	1/5/00	NA		55,000								
Warehouse	11/12/72	SL	4%	90,000	25,000	90,000		90,000		90,000		90,000
Land for warehouse	11/12/72	NA		32,000								
Equipment												
Boiler (80% man.)	1/1/01	SL	15 yrs	75,000	10,000	30,000	5,000	35,000	5,000	40,000	5,000	45,000
Air filter (100% man.)	7/2/03	SL	8 yrs	88,000	5,000	38,500	11,000	49,500	11,000	60,500	11,000	71,500
Water pur. (70% man.)	2/17/07	UOP	$.05/gal.	65,000	15,000		7,500	7,500	9,900	17,400	10,300	27,700
Extruder (100% man.)	12/20/07	UOP	$.09/unit	90,000	30,000		900	900	12,420	13,320	15,120	28,440
Minicom. (100% man.)	3/1/08	150DB	37.5%	45,000	30,000				23,438	23,438	19,336	42,774
Pack. mach. (100% man.)	3/30/08	DDB	66.6%	105,000	10,000				57,443	57,443	38,333	95,776
Heat syst. (80% man.)	4/30/09	SYD	15 yrs	95,000	20,000						7,917	7,917
A/C syst. (80% man.)	12/5/09	SYD	6 yrs	65,000	15,000						1,548	1,548
Vehicles												
Oldsmobile	11/3/04	SL	6 yrs	18,000	6,000	6,500	3,000	9,500	3,000	12,500	3,000	15,500
Delivery van (used)	1/14/05	SL	20%	20,000	5,000	8,000	4,000	12,000	4,000	16,000	4,000	20,000
Totals				1,143,000	271,000	243,000	41,400	284,400	136,201	420,601	125,554	546,155

Notes on the depreciation schedule:

- The newly acquired assets (heating system and air-conditioning system) are in boldface type.

- 2009 depreciation expense and accumulated depreciation are in boldface type.

- Land included in the purchase of the office building and warehouse is presented on the schedule even though it is not depreciated because most firms show *all* assets on their depreciation schedule.

- Although the warehouse was fully depreciated years ago, PlatCo continues to present this and all other assets the company owns on the depreciation schedule until the asset is disposed of.

- Assets used partly or entirely for manufacturing show the percentage of use allocated to manufacturing next to them so that anyone who reads the schedule will be able to make the year-end adjusting entries correctly. This is one of many ways to show the allocation.

- Note that the minicomputer and the packaging machine are being depreciated under the declining balance method. Even though this method uses the asset's declining book value rather than its depreciable base, the minicomputer and the packaging machine have their depreciable base and residual value listed separately because that is how the schedule happened to be designed. The acquisition cost of each asset is the total of these two items (depreciable base + residual value).

In computing depreciation for PlatCo, take the following steps to ensure that all of PlatCo's assets have been depreciated in 2009:

1. Add total depreciable cost and total residual value to yield the total acquisition cost of all assets that PlatCo is depreciating in 2009: To compute:

$1,143,000	total "depreciable cost or other basis" of all assets on the depreciation schedule
271,000	total residual value of all assets on the depreciation schedule
$1,414,000	total acquisition cost of all assets on the depreciation schedule

2. Subtract the acquisition cost of any assets on the 2009 schedule that were sold during the year. Because no assets on this schedule were sold during 2008, the total acquisition cost of all assets on the depreciation schedule is $1,414,000.

3. To verify the depreciation schedule, go to the general ledger, find all plant and equipment asset accounts and add all the balances (the balance in each account is the acquisition cost). The total should be $1,414,000. If the total of all depreciable asset account balances is more than $1,414,000, then somewhere is another asset that PlatCo has omitted. If the total is less than $1,414,000, then the schedule may list an asset that the company no longer owns, or there may be an error.

By including land on the depreciation schedule, you can quickly check the schedule against the general ledger asset accounts. If land had been left off the schedule, you would have had to add the balances of only the *depreciable* accounts, increasing the likelihood of errors and undermining the crosscheck.

Two adjusting entries are required to record PlatCo's depreciation expense for 2009. The first entry allocates depreciation for nonmanufacturing assets to the Depreciation Expense account. This entry will include depreciation for most of the depreciable assets. The second entry allocates depreciation for assets used in manufacturing to Inventory—Work-In-Process OH (overhead).

The data that you need to allocate depreciation was given on pages 126–127.

The first entry records depreciation in Depreciation Expense:

Depreciation Expense	22,983*	
Accumulated Depreciation—Buildings		10,000
Accumulated Depreciation—Equipment		5,983**
Accumulated Depreciation—Vehicles		7,000***

*$10,000	office building
1,000	boiler ($5,000 depreciation x 20% used for offices as noted on the schedule)
3,090	water purifier ($10,300 depreciation x 30% used for offices as noted on the schedule)
1,583	heating systems ($7,917 depreciation x 20% used for offices as noted on the schedule)
310	A/C system ($1,548 depreciation x 20% used for offices)
3,000	Oldsmobile
4,000	delivery van
$22,983	

**1,000	boiler ($5,000 depreciation x 20% used for offices as noted on the schedule)
3,090	water purifier ($10,300 depreciation x 30% used for offices as noted on the schedule)
1,583	heating system ($7,917 depreciation x 20% used for offices as noted on the schedule)
310	A/C system ($1,548 depreciation x 20% used for offices as noted on the schedule)
$5,983	

***$3,000 Oldsmobile + $4,000 VW van (used) = $7,000 for the vehicles

The second entry allocates depreciation in the Inventory—Work-In-Process OH account:

Inventory—Work-In-Process OH	102,571*
Accumulated Depreciation—Equipment	102,571

*$	4,000	boiler ($5,000 depreciation x 80% used for manufacturing as noted on the depreciation schedule)
	11,000	air filter (100% used for manufacturing as noted on the schedule)
	7,210	water purifier ($10,300 depreciation x 70% used for manufacturing as noted on the schedule)
	15,120	plastic extruder (100% used for manufacturing as noted on the schedule)
	19,336	minicomputer (100% used for manufacturing as noted on the schedule)
	38,333	packaging machine (100% used for manufacturing as noted on the schedule)
	6,334	heating system ($7,917 depreciation x 80% used for manufacturing as noted on the schedule)
	1,238	A/C system ($1,548 depreciation x 80% used for manufacturing as noted on the schedule)
	$102,571	

The total depreciation expense in these two entries should equal total depreciation on the schedule.

$ 22,983	allocated to Depreciation Expense
102,571	allocated to Inventory—Work-In-Process OH
$125,554	total depreciation taken for 2009 on the schedule

If PlatCo decides to sell or trade-in a partially depreciated asset, you must determine the asset's book value (acquisition cost – accumulated depreciation) to see if there is a gain or loss. To find accumulated depreciation for a particular asset, you can simply check the depreciation schedule. If you look in Accumulated Depreciation you will find total depreciation taken to date for *all* buildings, or *all* equipment or *all* vehicles rather than for the particular asset that was disposed of.

Revising the Estimated Life

It is not unusual for a company to discover that it has made an incorrect estimate of an asset's life or residual value. When this occurs, the company can revise the estimated life or the residual value and compute the new annual depreciation expense.

QUIZ 1   THE SUM-OF-THE-YEARS'-DIGITS METHOD OF DEPRECIATION

Problem I.

Multiple choice. Circle the correct answer.

1. Both the SYD and _____ methods provide more depreciation in the early years of an asset's life.

    a. straight-line method
    b. units of production method
    c. declining balance method
    d. all of the above

2. Under SYD depreciation, the sum of the years of an asset's life is determined by . . .

    a. adding up each digit that represents one year of the asset's life.
    b. applying the formula $\dfrac{n(n+1)}{2}$.
    c. either a or b.
    d. none of the above.

3. The sum-of-the-years'-digits for an asset with an estimated life of four years is . . .

    a. 24   b. 10   c. 5   d. 4

4. Depreciable base is the same as . . .

    a. market value.
    b. residual value.
    c. cost – accumulated depreciation.
    d. cost – residual value.

5. An asset has an invoice price of $26,000, sales tax of $1,400 and delivery charges of $600. Residual value is estimated at $4,000, and its estimated life is 5 years. If the asset is acquired at the beginning of the year and depreciated under the SYD method, depreciation for the *second* year is . . .

    a. $4,800   b. $6,400   c. $8,000   d. $11,200

Problem II.

An $18,000 machine with a residual value of $2,000 and an estimated life of 3 years is acquired at the beginning of the year and depreciated under the SYD method. What is depreciation for . . .

1. Year 1?

2. Year 2?

3. Year 3?

Problem III.

Complete the following table using SYD depreciation for an asset that has a cost of $35,000, a residual value of $1,500 and an expected life of 5 years. The asset was acquired on January 1, 20X1.

Year ending	Depreciation expense for the year	Credit to Accum. Depreciation	Year-end balance in Accum. Depreciation	Year-end book value
01/01/X1				
12/31/X1				
12/31/X2				
12/31/X3				
12/31/X4				
12/31/X5				

Problem IV.

A company acquires equipment on March 20, 20X1 at a cost of $75,000. If the asset has an estimated life of 4 years and is expected to have no residual value, compute SYD depreciation and the *balance* in the accumulated depreciation account for . . .

1. 20X1.

2. 20X2.

QUIZ 1 Solutions and Explanations

Problem I.

1. c

The declining balance and sum-of-the-years'-digits methods provide for greater depreciation in the early years and less in the later years. Straight-line depreciation results in equal depreciation each year, and depreciation under the units of production method varies each year with the level of production.

2. c

The shortcut for computing the sum-of-the-years'-digits is $\dfrac{n(n+1)}{2}$ where n = estimated life.

3. b

The shortcut for totaling the sum-of-the-years'-digits is the formula $\dfrac{n*(n+1)}{2}$ or $\dfrac{4(4+1)}{2}$ or $\dfrac{20}{2} = 10$

*n = estimated life.

4. d

5. b

First, determine the depreciable base by finding the acquisition cost: $26,000 invoice price + $1,400 sales tax + $600 delivery charges = $28,000 acquisition cost – $4,000 residual value = $24,000 depreciable base. To compute the denominator (SYD):

$\dfrac{5 \text{ years' estimated life } (5+1)}{2} = {}^{30}\!/_2 = 15$. At the beginning of the second year, 4 years of the estimated life remain, so depreciation for the second year is $^4\!/_{15}$ x $24,000 depreciable base = $6,400.

Problem II.

First, determine the depreciable base: $18,000 acquisition cost – $2,000 residual value = $16,000. Next, determine the denominator (SYD) of the fraction that will be used for the depreciation rate: $\dfrac{3(3+1)}{2} = 6$.

1. To compute depreciation for Year 1:
   At the beginning of Year 1, all three years of the asset's life remain. $\frac{3}{6}$ depreciation rate x $16,000 depreciable base = $8,000 depreciation

2. To compute depreciation for Year 2:
   At the beginning of the second year, only 2 years of the asset's expected life remain. $\frac{2}{6}$ depreciation rate x $16,000 depreciable base = $5,333 (rounded)

3. To compute depreciation for Year 3:
   At the beginning of the third and last year of the asset's life, only 1 year remains: $\frac{1}{6}$ depreciation rate x $16,000 depreciable base = $2,667 (rounded)

Problem III.

First, compute the depreciable base: $35,000 acquisition cost – $1,500 residual value = $33,500 depreciable base. Next, compute the denominator of the fraction used for the depreciation rate:

5 years' estimated life x $\dfrac{(5+1)}{2}$ or $\dfrac{5(6)}{2} = 15$.

Year ending	Depreciation expense for the year	Credit to Accum. Depreciation	Year-end balance in Accum. Depreciation	Year-end book value
01/01/20X1				$35,000
12/31/20X1	$\frac{5}{15}$ x $33,500 = $11,167	$11,167	$11,167	23,833
12/31/20X2	$\frac{4}{15}$ x $33,500 = 8,933	8,933	20,100	14,900
12/31/20X3	$\frac{3}{15}$ x $33,500 = 6,700	6,700	26,800	8,200
12/31/20X4	$\frac{2}{15}$ x $33,500 = 4,467	4,467	31,267	3,733
12/31/20X5	$\frac{1}{15}$ x $33,500 = 2,233	2,233	33,500	1,500

Problem IV.

To compute the depreciable base:
$75,000 acquisition cost – $0 residual value = $75,000 depreciable base.

To compute the denominator for the fraction used as the depreciation rate:

4 years' estimated life x $\dfrac{(4+1)}{2}$ or $\dfrac{4(5)}{2}$ = 10

Because the equipment was acquired on March 20, it is depreciated as if purchased on April 1 and is depreciated for 9 months ($\frac{9}{12}$) of 20X1. Because the depreciation rate is used for 12 consecutive months, the rate used for the last 9 months of 20X1 is also used for the first 3 months of 20X2.

1. Depreciation for 20X1 is $22,500.

To compute depreciation for 20X1:
4 years of the asset's life remain at the beginning of 20X1, so the depreciation rate is $\frac{4}{10}$. To compute: 4/10 x $75,000 depreciable base = $30,000 annual depreciation x $\frac{9}{12}$ = $22,500 depreciation for 20X1. The remaining $7,500 ($30,000 annual depreciation – $22,500 = $7,500 unused depreciation) will be taken at the beginning of 20X2.

The balance in the Accumulated Depreciation account at the end of 20X1 is $22,500.

2. Depreciation for 20X2 is $24,375.

At the beginning of 20X2, 3 years of the asset's life remain so the depreciation rate is $\frac{3}{10}$. To compute: $\frac{3}{10}$ x $75,000 depreciable base = $22,500 annual amount.

To compute total depreciation for 20X2:

$\frac{3}{12}$ (Jan.–Mar., 20X2) Year 1 x $30,000 Year 1 annual depreciation	= $ 7,500
$\frac{9}{12}$ (Apr.–Dec., 20X2) Year 2 x $22,500 annual depreciation for Year 2	= 16,875
Total depreciation for 20X2	$24,375

The balance in the accumulated depreciation account at the end of 20X2 is $46,875 ($22,500 balance from year-end 20X1 + $24,375 depreciation for 20X2 = $46,875).

QUIZ 2   **THE SUM-OF-THE-YEARS'-DIGITS METHOD OF DEPRECIATION**

Problem I.

Mark each statement True or False.

1. In the SYD depreciation rate, the numerator is the number of years remaining in the asset's life as of the end of the year for which depreciation expense is being recorded.

     a. True   b. False

2. Under SYD depreciation, depreciation expense declines each year.

     a. True   b. False

3. Residual value is not considered when computing SYD depreciation.

     a. True   b. False

4. When an asset is acquired in the middle of the year and depreciated under SYD, a new depreciation rate is computed each January 1 and applied for the entire calendar year.

     a. True   b. False

Problem II.

Complete the following table using SYD depreciation for an asset acquired on January 1, 20X1 at a cost of $80,000. The asset has a residual value of $1,000 and an estimated life of 4 years.

Year ending	Depreciation expense for the year	Credit to Accum. Depreciation	Year-end balance in Accum. Depreciation	Year-end book value
12/31/X1				
12/31/X2				
12/31/X3				
12/31/X4				

Problem III.

On July 1, 20X6, KupCo acquires equipment with an acquisition cost of $25,000, an estimated life of 3 years and a residual value of $5,000. Using the SYD method, compute depreciation for . . .

1. 20X6.

2. 20X7.

Problem IV.

You are given the following data for a computer purchased on January 1, 20X6:

Invoice cost	$5,500
Sales tax	$ 400
Delivery charges	$ 250
Installation and programming	$ 850
Estimated residual value	$1,000
Estimated useful life	3 years

Compute annual depreciation for 20X6, 20X7 and 20X8 under . . .

1. the SL method.

2. the DDB method.

3. the SYD method.

QUIZ 2 *Solutions and Explanations*

Problem I.

1. False
In the SYD depreciation rate, the numerator is the number of years of life remaining in the asset's life as of the *beginning* of the current year.

2. True

3. False
Residual value is used to compute the depreciable base (asset cost – residual value), which is multiplied by the SYD depreciation rate to yield depreciation expense.

4. False
When an asset is acquired in the middle of the year and depreciated under SYD, a new depreciation rate is computed one year from the purchase date and applied for the next 12 consecutive months.

Problem II.

First, determine the depreciable base: $80,000 cost – $1,000 residual value = $79,000 depreciable base.

Next, compute the denominator of the SYD fraction:

$$\frac{n(n+1)}{2} \text{ or } \frac{4(4+1)}{2} \text{ or } {}^{20}\!/_{2} = 10.$$

Year ending	Depreciation expense for the year	Credit to Accum. Depreciation	Year-end balance in Accum. Depreciation	Year-end book value
01/01/20X1				$80,000
12/31/20X1	4/10 x 79,000 = $31,600	$31,600	$31,600	48,400
12/31/20X2	3/10 x 79,000 = 23,700	23,700	55,300	24,700
12/31/20X3	2/10 x 79,000 = 15,800	15,800	71,100	8,900
12/31/20X4	1/10 x 79,000 = 7,900	7,900	79,000	1,000

Problem III.

First compute the depreciable base: $25,000 acquisition cost – $5,000 residual value = $20,000 depreciable base.

Next, compute the denominator to be used in the SYD fraction:

$$\frac{n(n+1)}{2} \text{ or } \frac{3(3+1)}{2} \text{ or } {}^{12}\!/_2 = 6, \text{ the denominator of the SYD fraction.}$$

1. $5,000 depreciation for 20X6.

To compute depreciation for the first 12 months:
$^3\!/_6$ x $20,000 = $10,000 depreciation for the first 12 months

However, the equipment was acquired on July 1, 20X6, so only 6 months of depreciation can be taken for 20X6. To compute: $10,000 depreciation expense for the first 12 months x $^6\!/_{12}$ depreciation permitted for 20X6 = $5,000 total depreciation for 20X6

2. $8,334 (rounded) depreciation for 20X7.

The depreciation for the first 6 months of 20X7 is the remaining $5,000 not taken in 20X6.

To compute depreciation for the last 6 months of 20X7, determine the new depreciation rate for the 12 months starting on July 1, 20X7. The new rate is $^2\!/_6$ (there are 2 years remaining on the asset's useful life).

To compute:
$^2\!/_6$ new depreciation rate x $20,000 depreciable base = $6,667 (rounded) depreciation expense for the 12 months beginning on July 1, 20X7 x $^6\!/_{12}$ (for the 6 months, July–December) = $3,334 (rounded) depreciation expense for July–December, 20X7

$5,000	depreciation for January-June, 20X7
3,334	depreciation expense for July-December, 20X7
$8,334	depreciation for 20X7

Problem IV.

First, compute the acquisition cost:

$5,500   invoice cost
   400   sales tax
   250   delivery charges
   850   installation and programming
$7,000   acquisition cost

Next, determine the depreciable base: $7,000 cost – $1,000 residual value = $6,000 depreciable base

1. Annual depreciation expense under the SL method is as follows:

    20X6 $2,000
    20X7 $2,000
    20X8 $2,000
             $6,000 depreciable base

To compute annual depreciation using the SL method:
$6,000 depreciable base/3 years' residual life = $2,000 annual depreciation expense

2. Annual depreciation under the DDB method is as follows:

    20X6 $4,667
    20X7 $1,333
    20X8 $ 0
             $6,000 depreciable base

To compute the DDB depreciation rate:

$$\frac{1.00}{3 \text{ years' estimated life}} = 33.33\% \times 2 = 66.67\% \text{ DDB rate}$$

To compute 20X6 depreciation:
$7,000 book value (DDB uses book value, not depreciable base) x 66.67% = $4,667 (rounded)

To compute 20X7 depreciation:
$7,000 book value – $4,667 accumulated depreciation for 20X6
= $2,333 beginning book value for 20X7 x 66.67% = $1,556
(rounded)

However, even though book value is used to compute annual depreciation expense under DDB, the asset still cannot be depreciated beyond the depreciable base of $6,000. To compute: $6,000 depreciable base – $4,667 depreciation taken = $1,333 maximum remaining depreciation. Thus, only $1,333 depreciation can be taken in 20X7.

Because the entire depreciable base has now been depreciated ($4,667 depreciation for 20X6 + $1,333 depreciation for 20X7 = $6,000 depreciable base), no depreciation can be taken in 20X8.

3. Annual depreciation under the SYD method is as follows:

20X6	$3,000
20X7	$2,000
20X8	$1,000

$6,000 depreciable base

To compute the denominator for the SYD rate fraction:

$$\frac{n(n+1)}{2} \text{ or } \frac{3(3+1)}{2} \text{ or } {}^{12}\!/_2 = 6$$

To compute depreciation expense for 20X6:
${}^{3*}\!/_6$ x $6,000 = $3,000

To compute depreciation expense for 20X7:
${}^{2*}\!/_6$ x $6,000 = $2,000

To compute depreciation expense for 20X8:
${}^{1*}\!/_6$ x $6,000 = $1,000

*years remaining in the asset's useful life

Section 7

DEPRECIATION UNDER FEDERAL INCOME TAX DEPRECIATION RULES

Important: **This section explains how to depreciate for tax purposes assets purchased in 2000 or thereafter. Prior to 2000, there were many changes in tax depreciation rules, rates and regulations. Therefore, for assets purchased before 2000, it is assumed that you will continue to use the depreciation methods, rates and tables on the company's tax depreciation schedules.**

Introduction

Under tax rules, most assets must be depreciated using the Modified Accelerated Cost Recovery System (MACRS, pronounced "makers"). MACRS requires few computations because IRS Publication 946, *How to Depreciate Property,* contains tables of depreciation rates. Because MACRS depreciation is based on the same basic concepts as GAAP, many companies use MACRS for both tax and book (financial statement) purposes if their statements do not have to undergo an audit or review, or if the difference between GAAP v. MACRS is not material.

However, MACRS does differ from GAAP as follows:

- ***Under MACRS, the entire acquisition cost is depreciated—there is no residual value.*** Under MACRS, a fully depreciated asset has a book value of $0. For example, if your company buys equipment with an acquisition cost of $150,000 and estimates a residual value of $25,000, the $150,000 cost is used to determine annual tax depreciation and the entire $150,000 is eventually depreciated, leaving a book value of $0. The company's estimate of a $25,000 residual value is ignored.

- ***Under MACRS, the IRS (not the company) determines the asset's life (recovery period).*** MACRS assigns all assets to specified class lives (recovery periods). Most assets, other than real-estate (real property), have a 5-year or 7-year recovery period, as follows:

  ✓ *5-year recovery period.* Includes computers and peripheral equipment (equipment controlled by the computer), automobiles, trucks, office machinery, typewriters, copiers, and adding machines.

✓ *7-year recovery period.* Includes office furniture and fixtures such as desks, files, chairs, safes.

Whether an asset has a 5- or 7-year recovery period also depends on the industry (see IRS Publication 946). If this publication does not list an asset as 5- or 7-year property, or does not list the industry that you want, ask a CPA to help find the proper recovery period. To compute annual depreciation for equipment using the MACRS tables, calculate the equipment's cost basis. Cost basis under tax depreciation is in almost all respects the same as acquisition cost under GAAP rules: invoice cost plus all costs required to put the equipment in service. When you have the cost basis, apply the depreciation rate from the appropriate MACRS tables in Publication 946.

- ***MACRS specifies the depreciation method for depreciable assets,*** as follows:

  ✓ *For equipment and most land improvements (but not buildings),* MACRS permits the straight-line or declining balance methods, but prohibits sum-of-the-years'-digits. Most companies choose declining balance to get the biggest expense (tax write-off) as soon as possible.

  ✓ *For buildings,* MACRS requires straight-line depreciation (in effect since 1987).

- ***MACRS stipulates how much depreciation can be taken in the first year, regardless of purchase date.*** This is different from GAAP depreciation, which depends on when the asset is purchased.

  ✓ *Generally, for first-year depreciation of equipment and most land improvements, MACRS requires the half-year convention.* This convention requires that all property (equipment and land improvements) be depreciated as if it were placed in service in the middle of the year, regardless of purchase date. For instance, if a company with a December 31 year end purchases equipment on January 1, MACRS requires that the asset be depreciated as if it were purchased on July 1, so that only one-half year of depreciation is taken in the first year. Similarly, if a company with a March 31 year end purchases equipment on April 1, MACRS requires that the asset be depreciated as if it were purchased on October 1 (the halfway point of the company's fiscal year).

  ✓ *For depreciation of buildings, MACRS imposes the mid-month convention.* This convention requires that buildings be depreciated as if purchased in the middle of the month, regardless of when actually purchased. For example, if a company with a December 31 year end purchases a building on January 1 and places it in service the same day or on the last day of the month, the company still takes 11½ months' depreciation for the first year. Similarly, if a company with an April 30 year end purchases a building on May 1 and places it in service the same day or on the last day of the month, the company also takes 11½ months' depreciation for the first year.

✓ *For depreciation of "passenger" autos, MACRS limits the annual amount* (explained in Section 8). GAAP does not have these limits.

- **MACRS tables in Publication 946 give each year's depreciation rate.**

TABLE 1. Equipment (partial IRS table)
(Half-Year Convention, 200% Declining Balance)

Year	3-year	5-year	7-year
1	33.33%	20.00%	14.29%
2	44.45%	32.00%	24.49%
3	14.81%	19.20%	17.49%
4	7.41%	11.52%	12.49%
5		11.52%	8.93%
6		5.76%	8.92%
7			8.93%
8			4.46%
Total Depreciation	100%	100%	100%

Table 1 uses the double-declining balance method, referred to in tax as "MACRS 200% depreciation"—then changes to straight-line to maximize tax depreciation in later years. The rate for Year 1 has the half-year convention factored in, and the rates for subsequent years have the asset's change in book value factored in. Thus, to find tax depreciation for a particular year, simply multiply the asset's cost basis by that year's rate.

For example, FisCo purchases* for $150,000 equipment with a 3-year recovery period. To compute first-year depreciation, find on Table 1 the 3-year property column, then find the rate for Year 1: 33.33%. To compute depreciation for Year 1: $150,000 acquisition cost x 33.33% Year 1 depreciation rate = $50,000 (rounded) Year 1 depreciation. The computation is the same whether the asset acquired is new or used.

*Under both GAAP and tax law, depreciation cannot begin until the asset has been acquired *and* placed in service. However, to avoid cumbersome, repetitious language ("acquires and places in service . . ."), it is assumed throughout this course that the acquired asset is placed in service on the date of purchase.

PROBLEM 1: Depreciation of 5-year property. On June 1, 2007, DryCo, which has a December 31 year end, purchases a new computer for $150,000. DryCo estimates that the computer will have a 10-year life and a $25,000 residual value. What is the total tax depreciation if the computer is new v. used for Year 1? for Year 2? for the remaining years of the recovery period?

SOLUTION 1: Purchase of a new computer.

The computations that follow are the same whether the acquired computer is new or used. To compute Year 1 depreciation:

Step 1. Determine the cost basis. It is the acquisition cost: $150,000 (given).

Step 2. Use the 5-year property column in Table 1. DryCo's estimate of a 10-year life is irrelevant.

Step 3. Compute Year 1 depreciation: $150,000 cost basis x 20% Year 1 depreciation rate for 5-year property = $30,000 Year 1 depreciation.

To compute Year 2 depreciation: $150,000 cost basis x 32% Year 2 rate = $48,000 depreciation for Year 2.

Total depreciation for the recovery period:

(Amounts may be rounded)

Year	Cost basis	x	Depreciation rate*	=	Annual depreciation
1	$150,000	x	20.00%	=	$ 30,000
2	150,000	x	32.00	=	48,000
3	150,000	x	19.20	=	28,800
4	150,000	x	11.52	=	17,280
5	150,000	x	11.52	=	17,280
6	150,000	x	5.76	=	8,640
Total depreciation					**$150,000**

*Table 1 depreciation rates for 5-year property.

Key points for Problem 1:

- Depreciation for tax purposes is computed using the cost basis, unlike depreciation for book purposes, which uses the depreciable base.

- The depreciation rate for Year 1 has the half-year convention factored in.

- Each year's depreciation rate is taken from the 5-year column of Table 1 because computers are 5-year property.

- Even though MACRS 200% depreciation is used, there is no need to compute each year's book value because Table 1 depreciation rates take into account the asset's declining book value.

- Although the asset is 5-year property, it is depreciated over 6 years because only one-half year of depreciation is taken in Year 1, leaving one-half year of depreciation to be taken in Year 6.

PROBLEM 2: Depreciation of 7-year property. On August 9, 2007, WyCo, which has a December 31 year end, purchases used equipment for $150,000. WyCo estimates that the equipment will have a 10-year life and a $25,000 residual value. What is the total tax depreciation for Year 1? for Year 2? for the remaining years of the recovery period?

SOLUTION 2: WyCo purchases used equipment.

The computations that follow are the same whether the acquired computer is new or used. To compute Year 1 depreciation:

Step 1. Determine the cost basis. It is the acquisition cost: $150,000 (given).

Step 2. Find the 7-year property column in Table 1. WyCo's estimate of a 10-year life is irrelevant.

Step 3. Compute Year 1 depreciation: $150,000 cost basis x 14.29% Year 1 rate for 7-year property = $21,435 Year 1 depreciation.

To compute Year 2 depreciation: $150,000 cost basis x 24.49% Year 2 rate (Table 1) = $36,735 Year 2 depreciation.

Total depreciation for the remaining years:

(Amounts may be rounded)

Year	Cost basis	x	Depreciation rate*	=	Annual depreciation
1	$150,000	x	14.29%	=	$ 21,435
2	150,000	x	24.49	=	36,735
3	150,000	x	17.49	=	26,235
4	150,000	x	12.49	=	18,735
5	150,000	x	8.93	=	13,395
6	150,000	x	8.92	=	13,380
7	150,000	x	8.93	=	13,395
8	150,000	x	4.46	=	6,690
Total depreciation					$150,000

* Table 1 depreciation rates for 7-year property.

Key points for Problem 2:

- The acquisition cost of $150,000 is the cost basis used throughout the furniture's recovery period.

- Even though MACRS 200% depreciation is used, there is no need to compute each year's book value because Table 1 depreciation rates factor in the asset's declining book value.

- Although the equipment is 7-year property, it is depreciated over 8 years, because only one-half year of depreciation is taken in Year 1 (already factored into the Year 1 rate in Table 1), leaving one-half year of depreciation to be taken in Year 8.

Depreciating Buildings Under MACRS

The cost basis of a building is the cost (not including land) plus all additional costs required to put the building in service. Recovery periods for buildings are as follows:

- 39 years for nonresidential (commercial) property such as offices, warehouses, and factories (Publication 946, Table 2).

- 27.5 years for residential rental property (Publication 946, Table 3).

Both Tables 2 and 3 use the straight-line method, and each month's rate has the mid-month convention factored in. Thus, the task in depreciating buildings is simply finding the right table in Publication 946.

PROBLEM 3: Depreciation of a commercial building under MACRS. MallCo, which has a December 31 year end, purchases an office building with a cost basis of $100,000, excluding land. The company estimates a $5,000 residual value and a useful life of 35 years. If the building is purchased on October 5, what is the depreciation for Year 1? Years 2-39? Year 40?

SOLUTION 3: *Step 1.* Determine the building's cost basis: $100,000 (given).

Step 2. Find the appropriate MACRS table in Publication 946. There are two MACRS tables for buildings, one for residential property (27.5-year property) and one for nonresidential property (39-year property). Below is the table for 39-year property that MallCo needs to depreciate its office building for tax purposes. The company's estimates of a 35-year life and a $5,000 residual value are ignored for tax purposes.

TABLE 2. Non-Residential Real Property
Mid-Month Convention
Straight Line—39 Years

Year	Month property placed in service											
	1	**2**	**3**	**4**	**5**	**6**	**7**	**8**	**9**	**10**	**11**	**12**
1	2.461%	2.247%	2.033%	1.819%	1.605%	1.391%	1.177%	0.963%	0.749%	0.535%	0.321%	0.107%
2–39	2.564	2.564	2.564	2.564	2.564	2.564	2.564	2.564	2.564	2.564	2.564	2.564
40	0.107	0.321	0.535	0.749	0.963	1.177	1.391	1.605	1.819	2.033	2.247	2.461

Step 3. To find the proper depreciation rate, choose the month in which the building was purchased and multiply the cost basis by that month's depreciation rate.

<u>To compute depreciation for Year 1</u>:
$100,000 cost basis x 0.535% depreciation rate (the rate in Column 10 because the building was purchased in October, the 10th month) = $535 first-year depreciation.

<u>To compute depreciation for Years 2-39</u>:
$100,000 cost basis x 2.564% (Years 2-39 percentage rate for a building purchased in the 10th month) = $2,564 depreciation per year in Years 2-39

<u>To compute depreciation for Year 40</u>:
$100,000 cost basis x 2.033% (Year 40 percentage rate for a building purchased in the 10th month) = $2,033 annual depreciation for Year 40

Total depreciation for the building equals its cost basis: To compute:

$ 535	Year 1
97,432	Years 2–39 ($2,564/year x 38 years)
2,033	Year 40
$100,000	Total depreciation

Reminders:

- Because the building was purchased in the 10th month of the year, you use the percentage rate in Column 10 every time you want to determine depreciation expense. **Important:** If your company had a June 30 year end and purchased the building on April 5, you would also use the percentage rate in Column 10 every time you wanted to determine depreciation expense, because April would be the 10th month of your company's fiscal year.

- The depreciation rate takes into account the mid-month convention in Year 1 and the effect that this has on subsequent years.

- Total depreciation for the recovery period equals the cost basis (acquisition cost). The company's estimated salvage value is irrelevant because tax rules permit depreciation of the entire cost basis.

- Although the asset has a 39-year recovery period, the company took depreciation for 40 years because $2\frac{1}{2}$ months was depreciated in Year 1, leaving $9\frac{1}{2}$ months of depreciation for Year 40.

**TABLE 3. Residential Rental Property
Mid-Month Convention
Straight Line—27.5 Years**

Year	Month Property Placed in Service											
	1	**2**	**3**	**4**	**5**	**6**	**7**	**8**	**9**	**10**	**11**	**12**
1	3.485%	3.182%	2.879%	2.576%	2.273%	1.970%	1.667%	1.364%	1.061%	0.758%	0.455%	0.152%
2–9	3.636	3.636	3.636	3.636	3.636	3.636	3.636	3.636	3.636	3.636	3.636	3.636
10	3.637	3.637	3.637	3.637	3.637	3.637	3.636	3.636	3.636	3.636	3.636	3.636
11	3.636	3.636	3.636	3.636	3.636	3.636	3.637	3.637	3.637	3.637	3.637	3.637
12	3.637	3.637	3.637	3.637	3.637	3.637	3.636	3.636	3.636	3.636	3.636	3.636
13	3.636	3.636	3.636	3.636	3.636	3.636	3.637	3.637	3.637	3.637	3.637	3.637
14	3.637	3.637	3.637	3.637	3.637	3.637	3.636	3.636	3.636	3.636	3.636	3.636
15	3.636	3.636	3.636	3.636	3.636	3.636	3.637	3.637	3.637	3.637	3.637	3.637
16	3.637	3.637	3.637	3.637	3.637	3.637	3.636	3.636	3.636	3.636	3.636	3.636
17	3.636	3.636	3.636	3.636	3.636	3.636	3.637	3.637	3.637	3.637	3.637	3.637
18	3.637	3.637	3.637	3.637	3.637	3.637	3.636	3.636	3.636	3.636	3.636	3.636
19	3.636	3.636	3.636	3.636	3.636	3.636	3.637	3.637	3.637	3.637	3.637	3.637
20	3.637	3.637	3.637	3.637	3.637	3.637	3.636	3.636	3.636	3.636	3.636	3.636
21	3.636	3.636	3.636	3.636	3.636	3.636	3.637	3.637	3.637	3.637	3.637	3.637
22	3.637	3.637	3.637	3.637	3.637	3.637	3.636	3.636	3.636	3.636	3.636	3.636
23	3.636	3.636	3.636	3.636	3.636	3.636	3.637	3.637	3.637	3.637	3.637	3.637
24	3.637	3.637	3.637	3.637	3.637	3.637	3.636	3.636	3.636	3.636	3.636	3.636
25	3.636	3.636	3.636	3.636	3.636	3.636	3.637	3.637	3.637	3.637	3.637	3.637
26	3.637	3.637	3.637	3.637	3.637	3.637	3.636	3.636	3.636	3.636	3.636	3.636
27	3.636	3.636	3.636	3.636	3.636	3.636	3.637	3.637	3.637	3.637	3.637	3.637
28	1.970	2.273	2.576	2.879	3.182	3.485	3.636	3.636	3.636	3.636	3.636	3.636
29							0.152	0.455	0.758	1.061	1.364	1.667

PROBLEM 4: Depreciation of a residential rental building under MACRS.
HomeCo, which has a March 31 year end, acquires a residential apartment building that has a cost basis of $100,000 (excluding land cost). The company estimates a $5,000 residual value and a useful life of 35 years. If HomeCo purchases the building on September 5, what is depreciation for Year 1? Years 2–9? Year 10?

SOLUTION 4: *Step 1.* Determine the building's cost basis: $100,000 (given).

Step 2. Find the proper MACRS table in IRS Publication 946. The correct one is MACRS Table 3, Residential Rental Property, 27.5-year recovery period (see page 153).

Step 3. For depreciation, find the month in which the building was purchased, and multiply the cost basis by that month's depreciation rate.

<u>To compute depreciation for Year 1</u>:
$100,000 cost basis x 1.970% depreciation rate (the rate in Column 6 because the building was purchased in September, the 6th month of the company's fiscal year) = $1,970 first-year depreciation

<u>To compute depreciation for Years 2–9</u>:
$100,000 cost basis x 3.636% (Years 2–9 percentage rate for a building purchased in the 6th month of the company's fiscal year) = $3,636 annual depreciation for Years 2–9

<u>To compute depreciation for Year 10</u>:
$100,000 cost basis x 3.637% (Year 10 percentage rate for a building purchased in the 6th month of the company's fiscal year) = $3,637 depreciation rate for Year 10

Note that for Years 10-29, there is a (very slight) difference in the depreciation rate for each year, unlike nonresidential property, which has only three depreciation rates for a building: Year 1, Years 2–39 and Year 40.

Special First-Year Expensing for Equipment: Sec. 179

MACRS rules allow a company to deduct (rather than depreciate over several years) in the year of purchase up to $125,000 of the equipment cost for the 2007 tax year (adjusted each year for inflation).* This provision is found in Internal Revenue Code Sec. 179 and is referred to simply as "Sec. 179." A company "elects" to take Sec. 179 on Form 4562. The equipment can be new or used, and a company can choose the equipment on which it wants to take the Sec. 179 deduction.

---

*A "tax year" is the calendar year in which the taxpayer's tax year *begins*. For example, if a company's fiscal year is April 1, 2006, to March 31, 2007, the company's tax year is 2006. If this company acquired equipment in February 2007, it could deduct only $108,000 of the cost under Sec. 179 because the equipment is being acquired in the company's 2006 tax year (when the Sec. 179 deduction was $108,000). Throughout this Section, where an example describes a purchase in 2007, it is assumed that the company's tax year is also 2007.

For example, say that during 2007, your company acquires Machine A for $125,000 and Machine B for $120,000. You can expense all $125,000 for Machine A or expense $75,000 for Machine A and $50,000 for Machine B, or use any other combination of expensing up to $125,000—then depreciate any amount not expensed for one or both machines. (Important: The election cannot be used for buildings, but can be used for improvements to real property, for which you should consult a CPA. Also, for practical reasons, it is rarely used for autos, as explained in Section 8.)

For example, on May 10, 2007, FisCo purchases for $126,000 tools with a 3-year recovery period and elects to take a full 2007 Sec. 179 deduction. Here are the steps it must follow:

First, FisCo takes the Sec. 179 deduction: $126,000 acquisition cost – $125,000 maximum Sec. 179 deduction for 2007 = $1,000 remaining basis.

Second, FisCo determines normal depreciation for 2007 by applying the Table 1 rate for 3-year property: $1,000 new cost basis x 33.33% Year 1 rate for 3-year property = $333 depreciation for Year 1.

Third, FisCo computes its total tax deduction for the equipment in 2007: $125,000 Sec. 179 deduction + $333 normal Year 1 depreciation = $125,333 total tax deduction for the equipment in 2007.

Note: Special rules apply for qualified New York Liberty Zone property, Qualified Enterprise Zone, Qualified Renewal Community property, and Gulf Opportunity (GO) Zone property as well as cost of advanced mine safety equipment.

PROBLEM 5: Taking both a Sec. 179 deduction and depreciation.
On July 12, 2007, ZelCo, which has a December 31 year end, purchases for $130,000 a new machine with a 5-year recovery period. If the company elects to take the full Sec. 179 deduction in the first year, what is the company's total tax deduction for Year 2? for the remaining years?

SOLUTION 5: Purchase of a new machine.

The computations that follow are the same whether the acquired machine is new or used.

Step 1. Determine the cost basis. $130,000 – $125,000 Sec. 179 deduction = $5,000 new cost basis to be used throughout the recovery period.

Step 2. $5,000 new cost basis x 20% Year 1 depreciation rate for 5-year property = $1,000 normal Year 1 depreciation amount.

Step 3. To compute total Year 1 deduction:

$125,000	Sec. 179 deduction for 2007
+ 1,000	First-year Table 1 depreciation
$126,000	Total Year 1 deduction

Depreciation for the remaining years:

(Amounts may be rounded)

Year	Cost basis	Depreciation rate	Annual tax deduction
1	$130,000		$125,000[1]
	5,000	20.00%	1,000
2	5,000	32.00	1,600
3	5,000	19.20	960
4	5,000	11.52	576
5	5,000	11.52	576
6	5,000	5.76	288
Total deduction for recovery period			$130,000

[1]Maximum Section 179 deduction for 2007.

To find an asset's book value, treat the Sec. 179 deduction as accumulated depreciation. Thus, at the end of Year 1, the net book value of the machine in Problem 5 is as follows:

For the new machine:

Asset (original cost)	$130,000
Less: Accumulated depreciation	(126,000)*
Net book value	$ 4,000

*$125,000 Sec. 179 deduction + $1,000 Year 1 depreciation for 5-year property from Table 1.

There are two important limitations to the Sec. 179 deduction.

Limitation #1

If a company purchases more than $500,000 of equipment (not including buildings) during the year, the $125,000 maximum deduction for 2007 is reduced dollar for dollar for any original cost basis over $500,000.

> **PROBLEM 6:** If GliCo purchases $528,000 of equipment during 2007, what is its allowable Sec. 179 deduction for 2007?
>
> **SOLUTION 6:** GliCo's allowable Sec. 179 deduction is $97,000. To compute:
>
> $528,000 original cost basis – $500,000 threshold = $28,000 excess. $125,000 maximum Sec. 179 deduction for 2007 – $28,000 excess = $97,000 allowable Sec. 179 deduction for 2007.

Limitation #2

A taxpayer may not claim a Sec. 179 deduction greater than its taxable income from any of its trade or business activities. In other words, a Sec. 179 deduction cannot be used to create an overall business loss on a current tax return. This limitation is complicated. Consult a CPA if a Sec. 179 election creates an overall loss for the year.

An Exception for Equipment: The Mid-Quarter Convention

The mid-quarter convention was created to prevent abuse of the half-year convention. The fear was that everyone would purchase equipment close to the last day of the year, then write off a full one-half year of depreciation.

The mid-quarter convention overrides the half-year convention when more than 40% of the aggregate basis of the equipment purchased—total acquisition cost for tax purposes less any Sec. 179 deduction—is purchased in the last 3 months of the taxable year. It does not apply to residential or nonresidential buildings, but may apply to some improvements to land. For improvements to land included in the mid-quarter purchase calculation, consult a CPA.

The following examples illustrate how this convention is used.

EXAMPLE 1: When the mid-quarter convention must be used:
In 2007, StimCo, a calendar-year company, makes the following purchases:

1. On January 15, Machine 1 is purchased for $25,000.

2. On June 25, Machine 2 is purchased for $25,000.

3. On December 31, Machine 3 is purchased for $175,000. StimCo elects to take a Sec. 179 deduction on this machine.

Must StimCo depreciate all equipment purchased in 2007 using the mid-quarter convention? To compute:

$ 50,000	purchased during first 9 months
+ 50,000	purchased during the last 3 mos. ($175,000 – $125,000 Sec. 179)
$100,000	total purchased during the year
x 40%	
$ 40,000	

StimCo must use the mid-quarter convention because the $50,000 of equipment purchased in the last 3 months exceeds 40% ($40,000) of the aggregate basis of all equipment purchased during 2007.

When the mid-quarter convention applies, the taxpayer cannot use the half-year convention but instead must use the mid-quarter convention.

EXAMPLE 2: How the mid-quarter convention is applied.
Because StimCo's purchases require use of the mid-quarter convention, it must treat each piece of equipment as though it were purchased in the middle of the quarter when the purchase occurred, as follows:

1. Machine 1, purchased on January 15, must be depreciated using the mid-quarter (instead of half-year) convention; that is, as if purchased in the middle of the first quarter. Thus, it will be treated as if purchased on February 15 and depreciated for $10\frac{1}{2}$ months (instead of for the usual half-year).

2. Machine 2, purchased on June 25, must be depreciated using the mid-quarter (instead of half-year) convention; that is, as if purchased in the middle of the second quarter. Thus, it will be treated as if purchased on May 15 and depreciated for $7\frac{1}{2}$ months (instead of for the usual half-year).

3. Machine 3, purchased on December 31, must be depreciated using the mid-quarter (instead of half-year) convention; that is, as if purchased in the middle of the fourth quarter (last 3 months). Thus, it will be treated as if purchased on November 15 and depreciated for $1\frac{1}{2}$ months instead of for 6 months (instead of for the usual half-year).

The exact amount of annual depreciation is provided in the tables in IRS Publication 946 (not shown here).

Generally, the mid-quarter convention results in less first-year depreciation than the half-year convention, as Congress intended. Only if a company makes significant acquisitions during the first quarter is it likely to have more first-year depreciation under the mid-quarter convention. To be safe, a company generally can avoid the mid-quarter convention by limiting fourth-quarter purchases to no more than 66.66% of the aggregate basis (that is, total cost basis) of assets acquired in the first three quarters (buildings are not included).

Note to Certified Bookkeeper applicants: Although application of the mid-quarter convention is not required for the *Certified Bookkeeper* examination, you must be able to determine when the mid-quarter convention applies (compute the aggregate basis of assets purchased and see if assets purchased in the fourth quarter exceed 40% of the aggregate basis of total equipment purchased during the year). The actual computation of depreciation is usually done by a CPA.

Completing the Depreciation Schedule at Year End

FamCo is a small, family-owned manufacturer and a calendar-year company. It uses tax depreciation for both book and tax purposes. During 2007, it purchases the following assets:

- On January 12, 2007, FamCo purchases for $250,000 a commercial office building. The purchase price includes land valued at $50,000.

- On May 25, 2007, FamCo purchases for $200,000 a new drillpress (7-year property), which will be used 100% for manufacturing.

- On November 10, 2007, FamCo purchases for $140,000, new equipment (7-year property), that will be used 70% for manufacturing and 30% for the offices. FamCo decides to take the full 2007 Sec. 179 deduction of $125,000 for the equipment.

Complete FamCo's depreciation schedule on page 161. Then record the adjusting journal entries at year end. Check your answers against the completed schedule on page 162 and the recorded journal entries on page 164.

Before attempting to complete the schedule and record the adjusting entries, you need to compute 2007 depreciation for the various assets. Try to do these computations before looking at how they are done below.

Computation to determine whether the mid-quarter convention applies:
$200,000 drillpress (the only asset purchased during the first three quarters of the year) + $15,000* equipment (the only asset purchased during the fourth quarter) = $215,000 aggregate basis of assets purchased during the year (buildings are not included in the mid-quarter convention computation) x 40% = $86,000.

*$140,000 equipment – $125,000 Sec. 179.

The mid-quarter convention does not apply because fourth-quarter purchases of $15,000 are less than 40% ($86,000) of the aggregate basis of all equipment purchased during the year.

To compute 2007 depreciation for the commercial building:
$200,000 cost basis ($250,000 cost – $50,000 allocated to land which is not depreciable) x 2.461% Year 1 depreciation rate on Table 2 (nonresidential property, page 153) originally acquired in the first month of the year = $4,922.

To compute 2007 depreciation on the drillpress:
$200,000 drillpress cost basis x 14.29% Year 1 depreciation rate on Table 1 for 7-year property = $28,580 first-year depreciation.

To compute Sec. 179 and first-year depreciation on the equipment:
$140,000 equipment – $125,000 Sec. 179 deduction = $15,000 new cost basis x 14.29% Year 1 depreciation rate on Table 1 for 7-year property = $2,144 first-year depreciation.

Depreciation Schedule (2007)

Methods
SL = straight-line
DB = declining balance
SYD = sum-of-the-years'-digits

KIND OF PROPERTY	DATE ACQUIRED	METHOD	RATE OR LIFE	DEPRECIABLE COST OR OTHER BASIS	RESIDUAL (SALVAGE) VALUE	DEPRECIATION IN PRIOR YEARS	DEPRECIATION FOR YR. ENDED	ACCUMULATED DEPRECIATION	DEPRECIATION FOR YR. ENDED	ACCUMULATED DEPRECIATION

Depreciation Schedule (2007)

Methods
SL = straight-line
DB = declining balance
SYD = sum-of-the-years'-digits

KIND OF PROPERTY	DATE ACQUIRED	METHOD	RATE OR LIFE	DEPRECIABLE COST OR OTHER BASIS	RESIDUAL (SALVAGE) VALUE	DEPRECIATION IN PRIOR YEARS	DEPRECIATION FOR YR. ENDED 12/31/07	ACCUMULTAED DEPRECIATION 12/31/07	DEPRECIATION FOR YR. ENDED	ACCUMULATED DEPRECIATION
Property										
Building	1/12/07	MM/SL	39	200,000			4,922	4,922		
Land for building	1/12/07			50,000						
Equipment										
Drillpress (100% man.)	5/25/07	HY/DDB	7	200,000			28,580	28,580		
200,000 x 14.29%										
Equipment (70% man.)	11/10/07	HY/DDB	7							
S. 179 deduction		179		125,000			125,000	125,000		
15,000 new basis x 14.29%				15,000			2,144	2,144		
Totals				590,000			160,646	160,646		

Notes for the depreciation schedule:

- There is no first-year bonus depreciation for the office building because buildings do not qualify for this.

- In the "Method" column, "MM" stands for mid-month (convention), "SL" for straight-line, "HY" for half-year convention, and "DDB" for double-declining balance.

- Land is included on the schedule even though it is not depreciated because most firms show *all* assets on the depreciation schedule.

- To make it easy to sum the "Depreciable Cost or Other Basis" column, two amounts are listed for the equipment: $125,000 Sec. 179 deduction, and the new cost basis of $15,000. These two amounts ($125,000 + $15,000) equal the original cost basis of $140,000, which is not listed to avoid duplication.

How can FamCo be sure that it has depreciated all of the company's depreciable assets? In other words, how can it make sure that an asset was not omitted from the schedule and therefore not depreciated for 2007?

First, FamCo subtracts from the "total cost or other basis" of $590,000 any assets on the schedule that were sold before January 1, 2007. There were none.

Next, FamCo verifies the depreciation schedule by going to the general ledger and adding up all the balances in the plant and equipment accounts (the balance in each account is the acquisition cost). The total should be $590,000. If the total of all depreciable asset account balances in the general ledger is more than $590,000, then FamCo has omitted an asset from the depreciation schedule. If the total is less than $590,000, then the schedule may list an asset that the company no longer owns, or there may be an error.

Why did FamCo include land on the depreciation schedule? Had land been omitted, the accounting department would have had to add the balances of only the *depreciable* accounts, increasing the likelihood of errors.

Two adjusting entries are required to record FamCo's depreciation expense for 2007. The first entry allocates depreciation for nonmanufacturing assets to the Depreciation Expense account, as follows:

Depreciation Expense	43,065*
Accumulated Depreciation—Buildings	4,922
Accumulated Depreciation—Equipment	38,143

* $ 4,922	office building
37,500	equipment Sec. 179 ($125,000 Sec. 179 for 2007 x 30% office use)
643	normal Year 1 depreciation for the equipment ($15,000 cost basis after Sec. 179 deduction x 14.29% Year 1 rate for 7-year property from Table 1 = $2,144 x 30% office use.)
<u>$43,065</u>	total 2007 depreciation allocated to depreciation expense

Note: You can record separate journal entries for Sec. 179 and MACRS, but in a busy office they are often recorded together. Anyone who wants to analyze the balance in Accumulated Depreciation for a particular year can review the depreciation schedule.

The second entry allocates depreciation for manufacturing assets to Inventory—Work-In-Process OH, as follows:

Inventory—Work-In-Process OH	117,581**
Accumulated Depreciation—Equipment	117,581

**28,580	drillpress depreciation ($200,000 original cost basis x 14.29% Year 1 rate from Table 1 for 7-year property)
87,500	equipment Sec. 179 ($125,000 Sec. 179 for 2007 x 70% manufacturing use)
1,501	equipment depreciation ($15,000 cost basis after Sec. 179 deduction x 14.29% Year 1 rate = $2,144 x 70% mfg. use = $1,501)
<u>$117,581</u>	total 2007 depreciation allocated to manufacturing

The total of these two entries should equal total depreciation taken in 2007 on the schedule.

    $ 43,065 allocated to Depreciation Expense
    <u> 117,581</u> allocated to Inventory—Work-In-Process OH
    <u>$160,646</u> total 2007 depreciation booked

If FamCo decides to sell or trade in a partially depreciated asset, you must determine the asset's book value (acquisition cost – accumulated depreciation) to see if there is a gain or loss. You can find the accumulated depreciation for a particular asset on the depreciation schedule (not in Accumulated Depreciation because the balance in this account may include depreciation for all the assets in that group, such as Accumulated Depreciation—Equipment).

When You See "Bonus Depreciation"

You may see on a company's depreciation schedule the phrase "bonus depreciation."

Companies that acquired qualifying assets after September 10, 2001, and before September 11, 2004, were *required* to take additional, or "bonus," depreciation of 30% in Year 1. To qualify for bonus depreciation, an asset had to be new and have a recovery period of 20 years or less—i.e., most machinery and equipment. Neither used property nor buildings qualified. If a company did not want to take this extra depreciation, it had to make a special election by filing Form 4562, *Depreciation and Amortization*.

First-year bonus depreciation was later increased to 50% for qualifying property acquired after May 5, 2003, and before January 1, 2005.

Before taking bonus depreciation, almost all companies took a Sec. 179 deduction. The computation was as follows: Deduct the Sec. 179 amount from the asset's cost basis to yield the revised cost basis. Deduct bonus depreciation from the revised cost basis to yield the new cost basis. Deduct normal depreciation using the new cost basis *starting in Year 1*.

Example 1. 30% bonus depreciation. On November 1, 2001, TorCo, a calendar year firm, purchased for $100,000 a new machine (5-year recovery period). What was TorCo's total depreciation for 2001? To compute:

$ 100,000	cost basis
− 24,000	Sec. 179 deduction for 2001
$ 76,000	revised cost basis
− 22,800	first-year bonus depreciation (30% x $76,000)
$ 53,200	new cost basis
x 20%	Year 1 depreciation rate for 5-year property
$ 10,640	normal Year 1 depreciation

To sum depreciation on the machine for the first year:

$ 24,000	Section 179 deduction
+ 22,800	first-year bonus depreciation
+ 10,640	normal Year 1 depreciation
$ 57,440	**total depreciation on the asset for 2001**

To depreciate the machine in Years 2-5, TorCo would multiply the new cost basis of $53,200 by the Table 1 depreciation rate for each year.

Example 2. 50% bonus depreciation. On June 1, 2003, TorCo purchased for $175,000 a new machine (5-year recovery period). What is TorCo's total depreciation for 2003? The computations are as follows:

$ 175,000	cost basis
– 100,000	Sec. 179 deduction for 2003
$ 75,000	revised cost basis
– 37,500	first-year bonus depreciation (50% x $75,000)
$ 37,500	new cost basis
x 20%	Year 1 depreciation rate for 5-year property
$ 7,500	normal Year 1 depreciation

To compute TorCo's depreciation for the first year:

$100,000	Section 179 deduction for 2003
+ 37,500	first-year bonus depreciation
+ 7,500	Normal Year 1 depreciation
$145,000	**total depreciation on the asset for 2003**

To depreciate the machine in Years 2–5, TorCo will multiply the new cost basis of $37,500 by the Table 1 depreciation rate for each year.

How bonus depreciation appears on TorCos' depreciation schedule. Below is a 2005 depreciation schedule showing Year 1 depreciation of the machine from Example 2, purchased on June 1, 2003.

Depreciation Schedule (2005)

Methods
SL = straight-line
DB = declining balance
SYD = sum-of-the-years'-digits

KIND OF PROPERTY	DATE ACQUIRED	METHOD	RATE OR LIFE	DEPRECIABLE COST OR OTHER BASIS	DEPRECIATION FOR YR. ENDED 12/31/03	ACCUMULATED DEPRECIATION 12/31/03	DEPRECIATION FOR YR. ENDED 12/31/04	ACCUMULATED DEPRECIATION 12/31/04	DEPRECIATION FOR YR. ENDED 12/31/05
Machinery									
Machinery (100% man.)	6/01/03	HY/DDB	7						
S. 179 deduction (2003)		179		100,000	100,000	100,000			
75,000 x 50% bonus				37,500	37,500	37,500			
37,500 new basis x 20%				37,500	7,500	7,500	12,000	12,000	7,200

The three amounts in the "Depreciable Cost or Other Basis" column add up to the acquisition cost of $175,000 as follows: $100,000 Sec. 179 deduction for 2003 + $37,500 bonus depreciation + $37,500 new cost basis = $175,000.

QUIZ 1   DEPRECIATION UNDER FEDERAL INCOME TAX DEPRECIATION RULES

Problem I.

Mark each statement True or False.

1. Under MACRS, one-half year of depreciation is allowed for equipment and buildings purchased in the first year.

    a. True   b. False

2. Under MACRS, an asset's life is assigned by the IRS rather than estimated by the company.

    a. True   b. False

3. Under MACRS, a calendar-year company will depreciate equipment (5-year recovery period) over 5 calendar years.

    a. True   b. False

4. Under MACRS, the half-year, mid-quarter and mid-month conventions apply to both buildings and equipment.

    a. True   b. False

5. The mid-quarter convention must be used when total equipment acquired in the fourth quarter does not exceed 40% of the aggregate basis of total assets (excluding buildings) acquired during the year.

    a. True   b. False

Problem II.

On September 3, 2007, StraCo purchases equipment for $145,000. Although the equipment has a 7-year tax recovery period under MACRS, the company estimates only a 5-year life. Answer the following questions using Table 1 on page 147. Assume that StraCo wants the biggest tax deduction it can get.

1. Given the company's estimate of a 5-year life, under which column will you find the correct depreciation rate, the 5-year or 7-year column?

2. a. What is the Table 1 depreciation rate for Year 1?
   b. What is the total tax deduction for the equipment for Year 1?

3. What is the depreciation rate if the equipment is purchased in January instead of September?

4. What is the Table 1 depreciation amount for Year 1 if the equipment has a $5,000 salvage value?

5. What is the net book value (see Section 2) of the equipment at the beginning of Year 2?

6. In Year 2, what amount do you multiply by the Table 1 depreciation rate of 24.49% to yield depreciation expense?

7. Complete the following table for depreciating the equipment. (In the first line of Year 1, put "Sec. 179" in the "Depreciation rate" column.)
   Give only one amount for the net book value in Year 1.

	Cost basis	Depreciation rate	Depreciation expense	Balance in Acc. Depreciation	Net book value
Year 1					
Year 2					
Year 3					
Year 4					
Year 5					
Year 6					
Year 7					
Year 8					
Total					

QUIZ 1   Solutions and Explanations

Problem I.

1. False
The half-year convention applies only to equipment. Buildings are depreciated under the mid-month convention.

2. True

3. False
Because of the half-year convention, only one-half year of depreciation is taken in Year 1. Then, a full year's depreciation is taken in Years 2–5, and the remaining one-half year (not taken in Year 1) is taken in Year 6.

4. False
Depreciation of equipment is determined by the half-year and mid-quarter conventions, not the mid-month convention. Depreciation of buildings is determined by the mid-month convention, but not the half-year and mid-quarter conventions.

5. False
The mid-quarter convention must be used only when total assets (excluding buildings) acquired in the fourth quarter *exceed* 40% of the aggregate basis of total assets (excluding buildings) acquired during the year. When the total basis of assets acquired in the fourth quarter does not exceed 40% of the aggregate basis acquired for the year, the mid-quarter convention does *not* apply.

Problem II.

1. The correct depreciation rate is found in the 7-year column. Under MACRS, the IRS has assigned the asset's life, called the recovery period in tax law. The company's estimate of the asset's life applies only to GAAP depreciation and therefore is irrelevant.

2. a.   14.29% (Table 1, Year 1, 7-year column)

2. b. $127,858
Deduction 1: $125,000 Sec. 179 deduction for 2007.

Deduction 2: $2,858 depreciation
To compute: $145,000 original cost basis – $125,000 Sec. 179 deduction = $20,000 cost basis after Sec. 179 deduction x 14.29% Table 1 depreciation rate (Year 1, 7-year column) = $2,858 Table 1 depreciation

Total deduction for Year 1: $125,000 Sec. 179 deduction + $2,858 Table 1 depreciation = $127,858 for Year 1

3. 14.29%
This is the Year 1 rate for equipment. The actual purchase date makes no difference (assuming that the mid-quarter convention does not apply). Under MACRS, the Year 1 depreciation rate takes into account the half-year convention, so that the 7-year asset is depreciated for only one-half year in the first year, regardless of the date of purchase.

4. $2,858
This is the Year 1, Table 1 depreciation amount, regardless of the salvage value. Under MACRS, the cost basis does not take into account salvage value.

5. The net book value is the cost less total accumulated depreciation to date. To compute:

Asset: Equipment $145,000   (original cost)
Accumulated depreciation: equipment ($127,858)   (Sec. 179 + Table 1 depreciation)
Net book value $ 17,142

6. $20,000
    Did you remember to use as the new cost basis the acquisition cost less the Sec. 179 deduction? To compute:
    $145,000 cost basis – $125,000 Sec. 179 deduction = $20,000 new cost basis to be used every year, starting in Year 1.

7. The following table shows how the equipment is depreciated:

		(Amounts and totals may be rounded.)			
	Cost basis	Table 1 depreciation rate	Depreciation expense	Balance in Acc. Depreciation	Net book value
Year 1	$145,000	Sec. 179	$125,000	$125,000	
	20,000	14.29	2,858	127,858	$17,142
Year 2	20,000	24.49	4,898	132,756	12,244
Year 3	20,000	17.49	3,498	136,254	8,746
Year 4	20,000	12.49	2,498	138,752	6,248
Year 5	20,000	8.93	1,786	140,538	4,462
Year 6	20,000	8.92	1,784	142,322	2,678
Year 7	20,000	8.93	1,786	144,108	892
Year 8	20,000	4.46	892	145,000	0
Total		100%	$145,000	$145,000	$ 0

QUIZ 2 DEPRECIATION UNDER FEDERAL INCOME TAX DEPRECIATION RULES

Problem I.

Multiple choice. Circle the correct answer.

1. Which of the following statements about MACRS Table 1 depreciation is false?

    a. An asset's recovery period is assigned by the IRS rather than by the company.
    b. In the first year, the company can elect a Sec. 179 deduction.
    c. Just one-half year of depreciation is allowed for equipment purchased and placed in service during the first year.
    d. The cost basis used to compute annual depreciation is the acquisition cost basis less salvage value.

2. On May 10, 2007, a company purchases equipment with a cost basis of $126,000 and takes a full $125,000 Sec. 179 deduction. That company . . .

    a. can both deduct the $125,000 and depreciate the remaining $1,000 of the cost basis in the first year.
    b. can deduct the $125,000 in the first year but must wait until the second year to start depreciating the remaining $1,000.
    c. must choose between taking the $125,000 Sec. 179 deduction and depreciating the $126,000 acquisition cost.
    d. must depreciate the full $126,000 acquisition cost without taking a Sec. 179 deduction.

3. Which of the following is *not* true about MACRS Table 1?

    a. The Year 1 depreciation rate takes into account the half-year convention.
    b. The depreciation rate for Year 1 is used regardless of the month of purchase.
    c. To compute depreciation, the cost basis is multiplied by the appropriate Table 1 depreciation rate.
    d. To compute depreciation, the book value is multiplied by the appropriate year's rate.

4. If you depreciate a nonresidential building under MACRS . . .

   a. you use MACRS 200% depreciation.
   b. you take 39 taxable years to depreciate a 39-year building.
   c. you select the depreciation rate in the column number that corresponds to the month of the company's fiscal year in which the building was placed in service.
   d. you select the depreciation rate in the column number that corresponds to the month of the calendar year in which the building was placed in service.

5. Generally, MACRS may be used to calculate depreciation for a company's financial statements . . .

   a. when the financial statements are to be audited by a CPA.
   b. when the financial statements do not require an audit or review.
   c. when the financial statements are prepared under GAAP rules.
   d. all of the above.

6. Which of the following statements is false?

   a. The half-year convention applies to equipment.
   b. The mid-quarter convention applies to equipment when more than 40% of equipment purchases are made in the last 3 months of the company's tax year.
   c. The mid-month convention applies to buildings.
   d. None of the above.

7. A company with a December 31 year end acquires $200,000 in assets in its first year: $110,000 for a machine in January and $90,000 in office furniture to furnish an entire building in October. If the company does not elect to take a Sec. 179 deduction, it will have to depreciate both assets using . . .

   a. the half-year convention.
   b. the mid-month convention.
   c. the mid-quarter convention.
   d. the Sec. 179 deduction.

Problem II.

On November 28, 20X1, QuipCo, which has a December 31 year end, acquires an office building for $250,000, which includes $50,000 for land. The building has an estimated life of 45 years and a residual value of $102,000. Answer the following questions using Table 2 (page 151).

1. What is the building's cost basis?

2. What is the depreciation rate for Year 1?

3. What would the Year 1 depreciation rate be if the building were purchased in February?

4. Fill in the missing amounts in the boxes indicated assuming that the purchase date is November 28:

	Cost basis	Table 2 depreciation rate	Depreciation expense	Accum. Depr.
Year 1	$200,000	0.321%	??	??
Year 2	??	??	??	??

5. What is the net book value of the land and building at the end of the second year (after the second-year depreciation has been recorded)?

Problem III.

On September 3, 2007, FranCo, which uses a calendar year end, buys used equipment, 7-year property, for $183,000. To maximize first-year expenses, FranCo takes a Sec. 179 deduction.

1. What is FranCo's total first-year combined deduction for Sec. 179 and depreciation?

2. What is the net book value of the equipment at the end of the first year?

3. What would FranCo's total first-year deduction (Sec. 179 plus depreciation) be if the equipment had been new instead of used?

4. Assume that FranCo had also purchased $140,000 in office furniture in October. What would FranCo have to do to avoid the mid-quarter convention?

QUIZ 2 Solutions and Explanations

Problem I.

1. d

Annual depreciation is computed using the full cost basis; salvage value is ignored under MACRS.

2. a

3. d

Each year, the appropriate depreciation rate is multiplied by the cost basis (total acquisition cost), not the book value.

4. c

Answer d would be correct only if the company were on a calendar year.

5. b

Generally, MACRS is not used when the financial statements are prepared under GAAP. The reason that this is "generally" the case is that when MACRS depreciation yields an amount so close to GAAP depreciation that there is no *material* difference, the MACRS amount can be used, even when the statements are reviewed or audited.

6. d

Answers a, b, and c are all true, but the question asks you which statement is false.

7. c

To compute:

$200,000 aggregate basis of assets purchased during the year x 40% = $80,000. The asset acquired in the fourth quarter has a cost basis of $90,000, which is greater than 40% of the aggregate basis of assets acquired during the year ($80,000), so the company must use the mid-quarter convention.

Problem II.

1. The building's cost basis is $200,000. To compute: $250,000 purchase price – $50,000 cost of land = $200,000 cost basis. MACRS, like GAAP, does not permit depreciation of land.

2. The depreciation rate for Year 1 is 0.321%. The building was purchased in November, the 11th month of the company's year, so the correct rate is found on the Year 1 line of the table in Column 11.

3. The depreciation rate for Year 1 would be 2.247%. February is the 2nd month of the company's year, so the depreciation rate is found in Column 2. The month in which a building is purchased affects the depreciation rate, unlike equipment, for which the month of purchase is irrelevant.

4. The correct amounts are as follows:

	Cost basis	Table 2 depreciation rate	Depreciation expense	Accum. Depr.
Year 1	$200,000	0.321%	$ 642	$ 642
Year 2	200,000	2.564	5,128	5,770

5. The net book value of the land and building at the end of the second year after depreciation is recorded is $244,230, as follows:

Asset: Building	$200,000	(original cost)
Less: Accumulated depreciation—building	(5,770)	(Year 1 + Year 2 depreciation)
Net book value	$194,230	
Asset: Land	50,000	
Net book value of property	$244,230	

Problem III.

1. **$133,288**

   To compute: $125,000 Sec. 179 deduction + 8,288 depreciation*
   = $133,288 (rounded) combined first-year deduction.

   *$183,000 cost basis – $125,000 Sec. 179 deduction = $58,000 revised cost basis x
   14.29% Table 1, Year 1, 7-year property = $8,288 (rounded).

2. **$49,712**

   To compute: $183,000 original cost – $133,288 accumulated
   depreciation ($125,000 Sec. 179 + $8,288 Table 1 depreciation) =
   $49,712 book value.

3. **$133,288**

   FranCo can take the same Sec. 179 and depreciation deductions
   regardless of whether the acquired equipment is new or used. When
   bonus depreciation was permitted, it was only for new equipment
   and machinery, so whether the acquired asset was new or used
   was important. But bonus depreciation is not permitted in 2007.

4. To avoid the mid-quarter convention, FranCo would have to apply
   the Sec. 179 deduction to its fourth-quarter purchase.

   Before taking a Sec. 179 deduction, the aggregate basis of both
   purchases is $323,000 ($183,000 third-quarter equipment +
   $140,000 fourth-quarter office furniture). FranCo's $140,000
   fourth-quarter purchase of office furniture would require FranCo
   to use the mid-quarter convention because $140,000 is greater
   than $129,200 (40% x $323,000 aggregate basis).

   To avoid the mid-quarter convention, FranCo must take a Sec. 179
   deduction on the office furniture. This will both reduce the basis of
   its fourth-quarter purchase to $15,000 ($140,000 original basis –
   $125,000 Section 179 deduction)—and reduce the aggregate basis
   of both assets to $198,000 ($183,000 third-quarter equipment
   purchase + $15,000 fourth-quarter office furniture purchase). Now,
   FranCo's fourth-quarter purchase of $15,000 of office furniture will
   not exceed $79,200—40% of its aggregate basis of $198,000 (40% x
   $198,000 = $79,200)—so the mid-quarter convention will not apply
   and FranCo can use normal Table 1 depreciation for both assets.

Section 8
TAX DEPRECIATION OF PASSENGER CARS AND OTHER VEHICLES

Introduction

There are special dollar limits on annual depreciation that apply only to a *passenger automobile*, defined under tax law as *"any four-wheel vehicle made primarily for use on public streets, roads, or highways and rated at 6,000 pounds or less of unloaded gross vehicle weight."* Thus, the special dollar limits apply not only to passenger autos, but also to light sport utility vehicles (SUVs), pickups, and vans.

There are no depreciation limits on the following vehicles:

- heavy SUVs, pickups, and vans with an unloaded gross vehicle weight *exceeding 6,000 pounds*

- specially modified light SUVs, pickups, and vans that weigh 6,000 pounds or less and are specially modified in a way to make personal use de minimus, such as seating only a driver and one passenger

- ambulances

- hearses

- taxis ("vehicles used in the trade or business of transporting people for pay or hire")

- delivery vehicles ("vehicles used in the business of transporting property for pay or hire") and trucks that are not designed to carry passengers

All of these vehicles, regardless of whether they come under annual IRS depreciation limits, are 5-year property (that is, they have a 5-year recovery period).

EXHIBIT A
Vehicles Placed in Service in 2007
(as published annually in IRS Publication 946)

	Passenger Autos	Light SUVs Pickups and Vans*
1st year	$3,060	$3,260
2nd year	4,900	5,200
3rd year	2,850	3,050
4th year and after	1,775	1,875

* Weigh 6,000 pounds or less, are built on truck chassis, and are not specially modified.

Depreciation Limits on Passenger Autos and Light SUVs, Pickups and Vans

Under MACRS, annual depreciation of a company car is computed in the same way as other 5-year equipment. But the amount of depreciation allowed each year is limited, as shown in Exhibit A above. There is one set of IRS limits for autos and another for light SUVs, pickups and vans (weigh 6,000 pounds or less) that are not specially modified.

In each year, you must compute Table 1 depreciation for the car, compare it to the IRS limits (Exhibit A above), and use the lower amount. **Important:** The IRS publishes this limit table each year, adjusting the limits for inflation. However, you must use the limit table for the year in which the car was acquired *throughout the car's recovery period.*

> **EXAMPLE 1:** During 2007, StudCo acquires[+] a new passenger auto with a cost basis of $28,000. What is Table 1 depreciation (see page 147) for Year 1? What is the IRS limit for Year 1? Which amount must StudCo use for its tax return? What is StudCo's maximum depreciation deduction for each subsequent year?

[+]Under both generally accepted principles (GAAP) and tax law, depreciation cannot begin until the asset has been acquired *and* placed in service. However, to avoid cumbersome, repetitious language ("acquired and placed in service . . . "), it is assumed throughout this course that the acquired asset is placed in service on the date of purchase.

	Cost Basis	x	Depreciation Rate (Table 1)	Computed Depreciation	IRS Limit (2007)	Tax Return Depreciation Expense	Depreciation Disallowed for the Year	Depreciation Deferred (Cumulative)
Year 1	$28,000	x	20.00%	$5,600	$3,060	$3,060	$2,540	$ 2,540
Year 2	28,000	x	32.00	8,960	4,900	4,900	4,060	6,600
Year 3	28,000	x	19.20	5,376	2,850	2,850	2,526	9,126
Year 4	28,000	x	11.52	3,226	1,775	1,775	1,451	10,577
Year 5	28,000	x	11.52	3,226	1,775	1,775	1,451	12,028
Year 6	28,000	x	5.76	1,612	1,775	1,612*	0	12,028
Year 7	28,000				1,775	1,775**	0	10,253
Year 8	28,000				1,775	1,775	0	8,478
Year 9	28,000				1,775	1,775	0	6,703
Year 10	28,000				1,775	1,775	0	4,928
Year 11	28,000				1,775	1,775	0	3,153
Year 12	28,000				1,775	1,775	0	1,378
Year 13	28,000				1,775	1,378	0	0
Total						$28,000		

*The company must use the computed depreciation of $1,612 because it is lower than the IRS limit of $1,775.

**In Year 7, the company can start to take the $12,028 in deferred depreciation that has been accumulating since Year 1. It can take up to the IRS limit of $1,775 per year until it has depreciated the full cost basis of $28,000. To allow for full depreciation of the cost basis, the recovery period is extended to 13 years.

To compute Year 1 depreciation:

$28,000 cost basis x 20% Table 1 rate for Year 1 depreciation = $5,600 total depreciation for Year 1. But the IRS Year 1 limit for a passenger auto (new or used) purchased in 2007, (Exhibit A) is $3,060. StudCo can take only $3,060 depreciation the first year. The $2,540 excess ($5,600 computed depreciation – $3,060 limit) will be taken in later years. The chart above shows tax depreciation over the auto's recovery period.

Why Sec. 179 Is Rarely Used for Passenger Autos or Light SUVs, Pickups And Vans

Under IRS Year 1 limits—$3,060 for an auto and $3,260 for a light SUV, pickup or van—there is no point in wasting part of the $125,000 Sec. 179 deduction, because it would exceed the deduction allowed.

EXAMPLE 2: As in Example 1, during 2007, StudCo acquires a new car for $28,000. As shown in Example 1, StudCo can take maximum depreciation of only $3,060, so there is no point in the company's wasting any part of the $125,000 Sec. 179 deduction on the car.

However, companies can and do take Sec. 179 deductions on trucks, tractors and other heavy vehicles.

Sec. 179 limits on heavy SUVs, pickups and vans.
For any SUV purchased after October 22, 2004, the Sec. 179 deduction is limited to $25,000. This rule applies to any 4-wheeled vehicle primarily designed or used to carry passengers over public streets, roads, or highways, which is not subject to the passenger auto limits, and is rated at no more than 14,000 pounds gross vehicle weight.

Exhibit B.
Summary of annual tax deductions for autos, SUVs, pickups and vans

	Section 179 deduction ($125,000 in 2007)	Depreciation
Passenger autos and unmodified light SUVs, pickups and vans	Rarely used	Apply the lesser of IRS limits or Table 1.
Trucks tractors and specially modified light SUVs, pickups and vans	Up to $125,000	Table 1
Heavy SUVs, pickups and vans	Up to $25,000	Table 1

The remaining cost basis after the Sec. 179 deduction is taken can be depreciated using Table 1.

> **EXAMPLE 3:** During 2007, StudCo purchases a heavy SUV with a cost basis of $27,000. What is StudCo's maximum tax deduction for the heavy SUV for 2007?
>
> To compute:
> $27,000 cost basis – $25,000 maximum Sec. 179 deduction for the heavy SUV = $2,000 new cost basis
>
> $2,000 new cost basis x 20% Table 1 depreciation = $400 Year 1 depreciation
>
> $25,000 Sec. 179 deduction
> + $400 Table 1 depreciation
> $25,400 maximum tax deduction for the heavy SUV in 2007.

When Employees Drive Company Vehicles for Personal Use

A company can treat a vehicle as though it were used 100% for business *even when employees drive it for personal use* under the following conditions:

1. the employer has a business reason for providing the vehicle, such as for business travel or as part of the employee's compensation as a perk for the job; and

2. the employer reports the value of the employee's *personal* use as taxable income on the employee's W-2.

> **EXAMPLE 4:** MatCo provides a passenger auto to employee Lee who periodically submits detailed records of business and personal mileage. For the year, Lee drives the car 80% for business and 20% for personal use. If MatCo includes the value of the 20% personal use in Lee's taxable income, the company can depreciate the car as though it were used 100% for business.

The Sole Proprietor's Company Car

A sole proprietorship (an unincorporated company with one owner), can depreciate a vehicle as though it were used 100% for business *even when employees drive company vehicles for personal use* under the same conditions:

> 1. the employer has a business reason for providing the vehicle, such as for business travel or as part of the employee's compensation as a perk for the job; and

> 2. the employer reports the value of the employee's *personal* use as taxable income on the employee's W-2.

But when the sole proprietor drives the car for personal use, there are different rules. Sole proprietors do not file a W-2 for themselves, so their personal use of their own car is not taxable income. However, they are allowed to depreciate the vehicle only in proportion to their business usage. For example, a sole proprietor who drives his or her own vehicle 68% for business can depreciate only 68% of the vehicle's cost basis for tax purposes.

> **EXAMPLE 5:** Sole proprietor Jane has a pickup and a car. She lets employee Rosa use the pickup for business and she uses the car. Mileage records show that she and Rosa both drove the vehicles 80% for business and 20% for personal use.
>
> - If Jane's company reports the value of Rosa's 20% personal use of the pickup as taxable income on Rosa's W-2, 100% of the pickup's cost basis can be depreciated.

- Jane does not report her 20% personal use of her own car as taxable income. Instead, she must limit her depreciation of the vehicle to 80% of the cost basis (because she used the car 80% for business). For example, if Jane's car has a cost basis of $20,000, she can depreciate only $16,000 ($20,000 cost basis x 80% business use). Her deduction of other vehicle costs (gas, repairs, oil, etc.) is also limited to 80%—the business use portion.

When a sole proprietor drives the car for both personal and business use, the IRS auto limit is also reduced by the personal use.

> **EXAMPLE 6:** In 2007, sole proprietor Jane purchases a car for $24,000. Mileage records indicate that Jane drives her car 75% for business use and 25% for personal use. Jane's cost basis is $18,000 ($24,000 original cost basis x 75% business use). What is Jane's maximum depreciation deduction for the auto on her 2007 tax return?
>
> To compute:
> $18,000 cost basis x 20% Table 1 rate for Year 1 = $3,600 Year 1 depreciation. However, Jane's maximum deduction, based on the IRS limit for a car purchased in 2007, is $2,295 ($3,060 x 75% business use). Jane's maximum depreciation deduction for the auto on her 2007 tax return is $2,295.

Because the depreciation schedule for a sole proprietor passenger auto that is driven partly for personal use is complicated, a CPA should be consulted.

Sole proprietors who use the company car do not have to include the value of their own personal use in their taxable income, but they must limit depreciation to the portion of the cost basis proportional to the business use of the vehicle. However, if a sole proprietor's employees drive the company car, their personal use is reported as personal income on their W-2, and the sole proprietor depreciates the full cost basis of the auto.

Depreciating Vehicles in Various Kinds of Companies

Here is a summary:

C corporations: The company can deduct 100% of the cost basis, provided that each employee's personal use of the vehicle is reported as taxable income on the employee's W-2. Some shareholder-owners may be subject to special rules.

S corporations: The company can deduct 100% of the cost basis, provided that each employee's personal use of the vehicle is reported as taxable income on the employee's W-2. Some shareholder-owners may be subject to special rules.

Partnerships: There are special rules for partnerships.

Sole proprietorships: The sole proprietorship can deduct 100% of the cost basis, provided that each employee's personal use of the vehicle is reported as taxable income on the employee's W-2. The owner's personal use is not reported as personal income. Instead, the percentage of the cost basis that is depreciated equals the percentage of business use for which the vehicle is driven. Thus, if a vehicle is driven 100% for business use, 100% of the cost basis can be depreciated. If the vehicle is driven 52% for business use, then 52% of the cost basis can be depreciated.

Completing the Depreciation Schedule at Year End

Because SmallCo is a small, family-owned manufacturer that does not need to show its financial statements to anyone, it does not bother with GAAP. It uses tax depreciation for both its tax return and financial statements.

During 2007, SmallCo purchases the following assets:

- On June 15, 2007, SmallCo purchases 10 used, specially modified Econoline delivery vans for $17,000 each, for a total of $187,000 and has the company name painted on each one. It will take a Sec. 179 deduction on the vans.

- On November 2, 2007, SmallCo purchases a new Lincoln passenger auto for $35,000.

Fill in SmallCo's depreciation for these assets on the depreciation schedule on page 187, then check your answers against the completed schedule on page 188.

Record the adjusting journal entries at year-end (remember that SmallCo uses tax depreciation for both book and tax purposes).

Determine whether the mid-quarter convention applies, then complete the depreciation schedule below and record the adjusting entries.

Before you can complete the schedule for 2007, you need to compute 2007 depreciation for the various assets. <u>Try to do these computations before looking at the ones below.</u>

To determine whether the mid-quarter convention applies:

$62,000* vans (the only assets purchased during the first three quarters of the year) + $35,000 Lincoln = $97,000 aggregate basis of assets purchased during the year x 40% = $38,800. Fourth-quarter purchases of assets ($35,000 for the Lincoln) do not exceed 40% ($38,800) of the aggregate basis of assets purchased during the year. The mid-quarter convention does not apply.

*$187,000 – $125,000 Sec. 179

<u>To compute 2007 depreciation for the vans</u>:
Because the vans are specially modified, they are not subject to either Sec. 179 limits or annual IRS depreciation limits. To compute: $187,000 cost basis – $125,000 Sec. 179 deduction for 2007 = $62,000 x 20% Table 1 depreciation rate for Year 1 = $12,400 Table 1 depreciation. $125,000 Sec. 179 deduction + $12,400 Table 1 depreciation = $137,400 total depreciation for the vans in 2007.

<u>To compute 2007 depreciation for the Lincoln passenger auto</u>:
$35,000 cost basis x 20% Table 1 rate for Year 1 = $7,000 Year 1 depreciation. However, the IRS Year 1 limit for a new car purchased in 2007 is $3,060 (see Exhibit A on page 180), so SmallCo can take only $3,060 depreciation on the Lincoln for 2007.

Depreciation Schedule (2007)

Methods
SL = straight-line
DB = declining balance
SYD = sum-of-the-years'-digits

KIND OF PROPERTY	DATE ACQUIRED	METHOD	RATE OR LIFE	DEPRECIABLE COST OR OTHER BASIS	RESIDUAL (SALVAGE) VALUE	DEPRECIATION IN PRIOR YEARS	DEPRECIATION FOR YR. ENDED	ACCUMULATED DEPRECIATION	DEPRECIATION FOR YR. ENDED	ACCUMULATED DEPRECIATION

Depreciation Schedule (2007)

Methods
SL = straight-line
DB = declining balance
SYD = sum-of-the-years'-digits

KIND OF PROPERTY	DATE ACQUIRED	METHOD	RATE OR LIFE	DEPRECIABLE COST OR OTHER BASIS	RESIDUAL (SALVAGE) VALUE	DEPRECIATION IN PRIOR YEARS	DEPRECIATION FOR YR. ENDED 12/31/07	ACCUMULATED DEPRECIATION 12/31/07	DEPRECIATION FOR YR. ENDED	ACCUMULATED DEPRECIATION
Vehicles										
10 Econoline vans (used)	6/15/07	179	5	125,000			125,000	125,000		
		HY/DDB		62,000			12,400	12,400		
Lincoln (passenger auto)	11/2/07	HY/DDB	5	35,000			3,060	3,060		
		LIM								
				222,000			140,460	140,460		

Notes for the depreciation schedule:

- In the "Method" column, "HY" stands for half-year and "DDB" for double-declining balance. (Many companies use instead "GDS," which stands for "General Depreciation System," a term commonly used to mean MACRS.) "LIM" stands for the IRS limit, referring to the fact that SmallCo could not take the computed depreciation.

The following adjusting entry will be required to record SmallCo's depreciation expense for 2007:

Depreciation Expense	140,460*	
Accumulated Depreciation—Vehicles		140,460

  *$137,400   11 vans
      3,060   Lincoln
  $140,460

If SmallCo decides to sell or trade in either asset before it is fully depreciated, the company will have to determine the asset's book value (acquisition cost – accumulated depreciation) to see if there is a gain or loss. SmallCo will use the accumulated depreciation amount found on the depreciation schedule—not the balance in Accumulated Depreciation—Vehicles, which probably also includes accumulated depreciation for all the vehicles that the company owns.

When "Bonus Depreciation" Appears on the Schedule

As noted in Section 7, companies that acquired qualifying assets after September 10, 2001, and before September 11, 2004 were required to take additional, or "bonus," depreciation of 30% in Year 1, and 50% if acquired after May 5, 2003, and before January 1, 2005. Although *new* vehicles qualified for bonus depreciation, it was irrelevant for passenger autos and certain light trucks and vans because of annual IRS depreciation limits.

Thus, on a depreciation schedule that includes those years, you are as likely to see bonus depreciation taken for trucks and other heavy vehicles as for machinery and equipment.

QUIZ 1   TAX DEPRECIATION OF PASSENGER CARS AND OTHER VEHICLES

Problem I.

Mark each statement True or False.

1. All company vehicles can be depreciated each year using the depreciation rates in Table 1 without limit.

    a. True   b. False

2. The Sec. 179 deduction is usually not beneficial for passenger autos, or light SUVs, pickups and vans.

    a. True   b. False

3. The same IRS limit applies in the first year of a passenger auto's recovery period, regardless of whether the auto is new or used.

    a. True   b. False

4. If an employee in a corporation drives the company car 70% for business and 30% for personal purposes, the company can still depreciate the car's entire cost basis.

    a. True   b. False

5. If depreciation for a passenger auto is computed using Table 1 depreciation rates and the amount is less than the IRS limit for that year, you have the option of using either amount for depreciation expense for the year.

    a. True   b. False

6. In 2007, you can take a Sec. 179 deduction for the entire cost of an SUV, pickup or van that has an unloaded gross vehicle weight exceeding 6,000 lbs.

    a. True   b. False

7. A sole proprietor who drives the company car 75% for business and 25% for personal purposes can still depreciate 100% of the car's cost basis.

  a. True   b. False

8. A sole proprietor whose employee drives the company car 75% for business and 25% for personal purposes may still depreciate 100% of the car's cost basis.

  a. True   b. False

9. Under the tax depreciation rules for passenger automobiles, a vehicle may be depreciated beyond the normal 5-year recovery period.

  a. True   b. False

Problem II.

Multiple choice. Circle the correct answer.

1. Which of the following vehicles does *not* come under the tax depreciation limits of passenger autos?

  a. An unmodified pickup weighing less than 6,000 pounds
  b. A company car used by the president
  c. A company delivery truck with 6 wheels weighing 8,000 pounds
  d. An unmodified company van weighing less than 6,000 pounds

2. When depreciating company vehicles under tax rules . . .

  a. depreciation limits on autos apply to all vehicles.
  b. depreciation is limited under GAAP.
  c. depreciation disallowed for a passenger auto during its recovery period can never be taken.
  d. a company auto driven by employees for both business and personal use is usually treated as used 100% for business when depreciation is computed.

3. Which of the following statements is true about depreciation under MACRS?

   a. A C corporation can depreciate 100% of a company vehicle's cost basis, provided that each employee's personal use of the vehicle is reported as taxable income on the employee's W-2.
   b. An S corporation can depreciate 100% of a company vehicle's cost basis, provided that each employee's personal use of the vehicle is reported as taxable income on the employee's W-2.
   c. A sole proprietorship can depreciate 100% of the proprietorship vehicle's cost basis, provided that each employee's personal use of the vehicle is reported as taxable income on the employee's W-2 and the owner does not drive the vehicle at all for personal use.
   d. All of the above.

4. Which of the following is likely to fall under 2007 IRS depreciation limits?

   a. An SUV weighing 7,000 pounds
   b. A 5,000-pound van that has several rows of seats and is painted solid white on the outside
   c. A 5,000-pound pickup with all seats removed except the one for the driver
   d. A semi cab

5. On April 25, 2007, CryCo purchases for $30,000 an SUV weighing 6,100 pounds. The maximum writeoff CryCo can take on this SUV for 2007 is:

   a. $30,000
   b. $25,000
   c. $26,000
   d. $3,260

QUIZ 1   Solutions and Explanations

Problem I.

1. False
   Depreciation for passenger autos and light SUVs, pickups, and vans is limited to amounts set each year by the IRS.

2. True
   The IRS limits on depreciation make the Sec. 179 deduction useless for most passenger autos.

3. True

4. True
   The corporation can fully depreciate the company car's cost basis even if an employee drove the car for personal use, provided the company reports the value of the employee's personal use in the employee's taxable income on the W-2.

5. False
   When depreciation computed for a car is different from the IRS limit, you *must* use the lower amount.

6. False
   In 2007, the Sec. 179 deduction for a heavy SUV, pickup, or van is limited to $25,000.

7. False
   The sole proprietor who uses the car 75% for business can depreciate only 75% of the cost basis.

8. True

Once again, the key word is "may." The sole proprietor *may* fully depreciate the company car's cost basis even if an employee drove the car for personal use—*if* the value of the employee's personal use of the car is included in taxable income on the employee's W-2.

9. True

Depreciation disallowed because of annual IRS limits is deferred and taken at the end of the MACRS 5-year recovery period, even if this requires extending the recovery period by several years.

Problem II.

1. c

Answer a, a pickup weighing less than 6,000 pounds, comes under IRS limits for light SUVs, pickups and vans that have not been specially modified. Answer b, a company car, comes under IRS limits for passengers autos. Answer d, a van weighing less than 6,000 pounds comes under the same IRS limits as answer a.

2. d

The company treats the auto as being driven 100% for business use even if employees drive the auto for personal use by reporting employees' personal use as taxable income on their W-2s.

3. d

4. b

Answer a, an SUV weighing 7,000 pounds would fall under the Sec. 179 limit of $25,000, but not under IRS depreciation limits.

5. c

Answer a, $30,000, is wrong because the maximum Sec. 179 deduction for a heavy SUV purchased in 2007 is $25,000. Answer b, $25,000, includes the $25,000 Sec. 179 deduction, but does not include Table 1 depreciation of $1,000 ($30,000 cost basis − $25,000 Sec. 179 = $5,000 revised cost basis x 20% Table 1 depreciation = $1,000). Answer d, $3,260, is the IRS limit on SUVs, pickups and vans that weigh 6,000 pounds or less—but the SUV that CryCo purchased weighs 6,100 pounds.

QUIZ 2   **TAX DEPRECIATION OF PASSENGER AUTOS AND OTHER VEHICLES**

Problem I.

On December 8, 2007, RimCo, which has a December 31 year end, purchases a new passenger auto for $32,000. Use Exhibit A (page 180) and Table 1 (page 147) to answer the questions below. Assume that the mid-quarter convention does not apply.

1. What is the calculated depreciation for the new passenger auto in Year 1?

2. Would the table amount of depreciation change if the auto were purchased in June instead of December?

3. What is the maximum depreciation that RimCo can take for the car in Year 1?

4. Must any Year 1 depreciation be deferred? If yes, how much?

5. What is the calculated amount of depreciation in Year 2?

6. How much depreciation can RimCo take in Year 2?

7. Must any Year 2 depreciation be deferred? If yes, how much?

8. At the end of Year 2, what is the auto's net book value on the company's balance sheet?

9. By the end of Year 2, what is the total amount of depreciation that has been deferred?

10. Fill in the missing amounts in the following table (page 196).

	Cost Basis	x	Table 1 Depr. Rate (5-year property)	Computed Depreciation	IRS Limit (2007)	Debit to Depr. Expense	Depreciation Disallowed for the Year	Depreciation Deferred (Cumulative)
Year 1	$32,000	x	20.00	$??	$3,060	??	??	??
Year 2	??	x	32.00	??	4,900	??	??	??
Year 3	??	x	19.20	??	2,850	??	??	??
Year 4	??	x	11.52	??	1,775	??	??	??
Year 5	??	x	11.52	??	1,775	??	??	??
Year 6	??	x	5.76	??	1,775	??	??	??
Year 7						??	??	??
Year 8						??	??	??
Year 9						??	??	??
Year 10						??	??	??
Year 11						??	??	??
Year 12						??	??	??
Year 13						??	??	??
Year 14						??	??	??
Year 15						??	??	??
Total						??	??	??

QUIZ 2   Solutions and Explanations

Problem I.

1. $6,400
To compute: $32,000 x 20% Table 1 rate, 5-year column, Year 1 = $6,400.

2. No, the table amount of depreciation would not change if the auto were purchased in June instead of December, because generally tax rules allow one-half year of depreciation for equipment, regardless of when it is purchased.

3. $3,060
The IRS first-year limit for a new car purchased in 2007 is $3,060, which is lower than the computed depreciation of $6,400. Under tax law, the lower amount must be used.

4. $3,340
To compute: $6,400 computed depreciation – $3,060 permitted Year 1 depreciation = $3,340 deferred.

5. $10,240
To compute: $32,000 cost basis x 32% (Table 1, 5-year column, Year 2) = $10,240.

6. $4,900
The IRS second-year limit on depreciation of $4,900 is lower than the computed depreciation of $10,240. Under tax law, the lower amount must be used.

7. Yes. $5,340
To compute: $10,240 computed amount – $4,900 limit = $5,340 depreciation deferred in Year 2.

8. At the end of the second year, the auto's net book value on the company's balance sheet is as follows:

Asset: Automobile	$32,000 (original cost)
Accumulated Depreciation—Automobile	(7,960) ($3,060 Year 1 + $4,900 Year 2)
Net book value	$24,040

9. $8,680

To compute:
$3,340 depreciation deferred in the first year
+ $5,340 depreciation deferred in the second year
$8,680 total depreciation deferred by the end of the second year.

10. The correct amounts are shown in the following table:

	Cost Basis	x	Table 1 rate (5-year property)	Computed Depreciation	IRS Limit (2007)	Debit to Depreciation Expense	Depreciation Disallowed for the Year	Depreciation Deferred (Cumulative)
Year 1	$32,000	x	20.00	$ 6,400	$3,060	$3,060	$3,340	$ 3,340
Year 2	32,000	x	32.00	10,240	4,900	4,900	5,340	8,680
Year 3	32,000	x	19.20	6,144	2,850	2,850	3,294	11,974
Year 4	32,000	x	11.52	3,686	1,775	1,775	1,911	13,885
Year 5	32,000	x	11.52	3,686	1,775	1,775	1,911	15,796
Year 6	32,000	x	5.76	1,844	1,775	1,775	69	15,865
Year 7					1,775	1,775		14,090
Year 8					1,775	1,775		12,315
Year 9					1,775	1,775		10,540
Year 10					1,775	1,775		8,765
Year 11					1,775	1,775		6,990
Year 12					1,775	1,775		5,215
Year 13					1,775	1,775		3,440
Year 14					1,775	1,775		1,665
Year 15					1,775	1,665*		0
						$32,000		

*Only $1,665 depreciation is left in Year 15 to reach the original cost basis of $32,000.

Final Examination (Optional)
MASTERING DEPRECIATION

Instructions: Detach the Final Examination Answer Sheet on page 213 before beginning your final examination. Select the correct letter for the answer to each multiple-choice question below and mark it in on the Answer Sheet. Allow approximately 2½ hours.

The following information may be needed to answer some questions.

Equipment (partial IRS table)
(Half-Year Convention, 200% Declining Balance)

Year	3-year	5-year	7-year
1	33.33%	20.00%	14.29%
2	44.45	32.00	24.49
3	14.81	19.20	17.49
4	7.41	11.52	12.49
5		11.52	8.93
6		5.76	8.92
7			8.93
8			4.46
Total depreciation	100%	100%	100%

Nonresidential Real Property
Mid-Month Convention
Straight Line—39 Years

Year	Month property placed in service											
	1	2	3	4	5	6	7	8	9	10	11	12
1	2.461%	2.247%	2.033%	1.819%	1.605%	1.391%	1.177%	0.963%	0.749%	0.535%	0.321%	0.107%
2–39	2.564	2.564	2.564	2.564	2.564	2.564	2.564	2.564	2.564	2.564	2.564	2.564
40	0.107	0.321	0.535	0.749	0.963	1.177	1.391	1.605	1.819	2.033	2.247	2.461

Vehicles Placed in Service in 2007

	Passenger Autos	Light SUVs Pickups and Vans*
1st year	$3,060	$3,260
2nd year	4,900	5,200
3rd year	2,850	3,050
4th year and after	1,775	1,875

* Weigh 6,000 pounds or less, are built on truck chassis, and are not specially modified.

> **NOTE: The maximum Section 179 deduction for tax years beginning in 2007 is $125,000.**

1. Under both GAAP and tax depreciation, an asset cannot be depreciated until it has been . . .

    a. acquired and placed in service.
    b. acquired (even if not yet placed in service).
    c. recorded on company books in an asset account.
    d. categorized by the company as being for office use, for manufacturing, or for a combination of both.

2. Companies whose financial statements are to be audited or reviewed by a CPA . . .

    a. can always use tax depreciation rules for their financial statements.
    b. can never use tax depreciation methods for their financial statements.
    c. can use tax depreciation for their financial statements if the difference between the amounts computed under GAAP and tax rules is not material.
    d. can sometimes use UOP depreciation for their tax return.

3. If a calendar-year company purchases more than $500,000 of equipment during 2007, not including buildings, the maximum Section 179 deduction of $125,000 is . . .

    a. reduced by the amount found in the appropriate IRS table.
    b. reduced dollar for dollar by the amount of equipment purchased above $500,000.
    c. eliminated.
    d. still permitted, but no depreciation can be taken for the year.

4. To calculate depreciation using GAAP rules, you must determine an asset's . . .

    a. acquisition cost, estimated life, residual value and the depreciation method to be used.
    b. cost basis and recovery period.
    c. cost basis, depreciable basis and recovery period.
    d. cost basis, depreciable basis, recovery period and the depreciation method to be used.

5. An asset's original cost includes . . .

    a. the invoice price, but not the sales tax or transportation or installation costs.
    b. the invoice price and sales tax, but not the transportation or installation costs.
    c. the invoice price, sales tax and transportation costs, but not the installation costs.
    d. the invoice price, sales tax and transportation and installation costs.

6. Regardless of the GAAP depreciation method selected . . .

    a. the maximum allowable depreciation over the asset's life is the same.
    b. the total accumulated depreciation at the end of the asset's life will equal the depreciable base.
    c. the total accumulated depreciation at the end of the asset's life cannot exceed the depreciable base.
    d. all of the above.

7. On August 1 of the current year, a company with a December 31 year-end buys a nonresidential building for $600,000, which includes land that costs $100,000. Under MACRS, depreciation for this year will be . . .

a. $14,766   b. $12,305   c. $5,778   d. $4,815

8. For the building in Question 7, depreciation in the 12th year will be . . .

a. $15,384   b. $12,820   c. $642   d. $535

9. When MACRS, Table 1 depreciation for a passenger auto or light SUV, pickup or van is in excess of annual IRS limits the excess depreciation . . .

a. is lost permanently.
b. may be taken by extending the MACRS recovery period for one extra year.
c. may be taken by extending the MACRS recovery period for as many years as are needed to depreciate the cost basis.
d. may result in the auto being depreciated under a GAAP method.

10. During 2007, your firm acquires a 5,000-lb. SUV for $30,000 and a 6,200-lb. SUV for $35,000. How much of the cost can you take as a Sec. 179 deduction in 2007, respectively?

a. $25,000 and $25,000
b. $0 and $25,000
c. $30,000 and $35,000
d. You cannot take a Sec. 179 deduction for SUVs.

11. The mid-quarter convention must be used when the aggregate basis of assets (excluding buildings) acquired during the last 3 months of the year . . .

a. exceeds 40% of the aggregate basis of assets (excluding buildings) purchased during the year.
b. is no more than 40% of the aggregate basis of assets (excluding buildings) purchased during the year.
c. exceeds 40% of the aggregate basis of assets (excluding buildings) purchased during the first three quarters of the year.
d. is no more than 40% of the aggregate basis of assets (excluding buildings) purchased during the first three quarters of the year.

12. The half-year convention generally applies to . . .

    a. all assets being depreciated under MACRS.
    b. assets other than buildings being depreciated under MACRS.
    c. assets other than passenger autos being depreciated under MACRS.
    d. assets other than buildings and passenger autos being depreciated under MACRS.

13. The mid-month convention applies to . . .

    a. assets purchased during the last 3 months whose aggregate basis exceeds 40% of the aggregate basis of assets purchased during the year.
    b. assets other than buildings purchased during the last 3 months whose aggregate basis exceeds 40% of the aggregate basis of assets other than buildings purchased during the year.
    c. buildings.
    d. buildings and land.

14. In units of production depreciation, the depreciation rate is calculated as . . .

    a. (acquisition cost – residual value)/total estimated units of production.
    b. (historical cost – salvage value)/total estimated units produced, labor hours used or miles driven.
    c. (depreciable base)/total estimated units of output.
    d. any of the above.

15. For new machinery or equipment acquired before 2005, the phrase "bonus depreciation" on a depreciation schedule would refer to first-year depreciation of either 30% or 50% taken . . .

    a. after the Sec. 179 deduction and before Table 1 depreciation.
    b. before both the Sec. 179 deduction and Table 1 depreciation.
    c. in place of the Sec. 179 deduction and Table 1 depreciation.
    d. after the Sec. 179 deduction and in place of Table 1 depreciation.

16. Under GAAP, annual depreciation for a building can be allocated . . .

    a. entirely to Depreciation Expense, entirely to Inventory—Work-In-Process OH or partly to both, depending on how the building is used.

    b. only to Depreciation Expense.

    c. only to Inventory—Work-In-Process OH.

    d. entirely to either Depreciation Expense or Inventory—Work-In-Process OH, but not allocated partly to both.

17. To depreciate an asset under the double-declining balance method, multiply . . .

    a. the depreciable base by each year's depreciation rate.

    b. the depreciation rate by each year's beginning book value.

    c. the acquisition cost by each year's depreciation rate.

    d. the cost basis by each year's depreciation rate.

18. Under straight-line depreciation, the annual depreciation rate is computed by . . .

    a. dividing 100% by the estimated life.

    b. dividing the numeral 1.00 by the estimated life.

    c. either a or b.

    d. none of the above.

19. Under sum-of-the-years'-digits depreciation . . .

    a. the book value remains the same each year.

    b. the depreciation rate changes each year.

    c. the denominator of the SYD fraction changes each year.

    d. all of the above.

20. For assets acquired during the year, the sum-of-the-years'-digits method requires that the same depreciation rate be used . . .

    a. for the remaining months of the year of acquisition, then again in the final year of the asset's estimated life for any months not depreciated in Year 1.

    b. for 12 consecutive months, even if that results in the same rate being used in two different calendar years.

    c. throughout the life of the asset.

    d. until the end of the calendar year, then recomputed for the next calendar year.

21. Company records show that an employee provided with a company car drove it 80% for business and 20% for personal use. The company reports the personal use as income on the employee's W-2. As a result . . .

    a. the company can depreciate 80% of the car's cost basis.

    b. the company cannot depreciate the car.

    c. the company can depreciate 100% of the car's cost basis.

    d. the company can depreciate the car without IRS limits on annual depreciation.

22. On which of the following assets can a company take a Sec. 179 deduction?

    a. a warehouse

    b. a computer

    c. a rental apartment building

    d. an office building

23. On August 10, 2007, a calendar-year company purchases a new machine (7-year property) with a cost basis of $195,000. Under MACRS, what is the combined first-year Sec. 179 deduction and depreciation (rounded) for the machine?

    a. $135,003   b. $90,000   c. $27,866   d. $10,003

24. Under MACRS, a sole proprietor who uses her own car 20% for personal purposes and 80% for business in her unincorporated company . . .

    a. can depreciate 80% of the car's cost basis.
    b. can depreciate 100% of the car's cost basis.
    c. can depreciate 20% of the car's cost basis.
    d. cannot depreciate the car if it is not used 100% for business.

25. A company pays $30,000 for two machines. Machine A is appraised at a fair market value of $24,000 and Machine B at a fair market value of $8,000. The cost of Machine B is recorded for book purposes at . . .

    a. $7,500   b. $8,000   c. $24,000   d. $30,000

26. On July 1, 2007, a calendar-year corporation purchases a used passenger auto for $15,000. The maximum tax depreciation allowed on the auto in 2007 is . . .

    a. $2,144   b. $3,000   c. $3,060   d. $3,260

27. For the asset in Question 26, maximum depreciation in Year 6 will be . . .

    a. $1,775   b. $864   c. $1,140   d. $3,000

Use the following information to answer Questions 28–30: On January 2, 2007, a company purchases a machine for $11,000 and estimates that it will have a 10-year life and a residual value of $1,000. It is depreciating the machine for book purposes under the straight-line method.

28. What is the journal entry to record Year 1 depreciation for a nonmanufacturing company?

    a. Depreciation Expense   1,000
          Accumulated Depreciation—Machine   1,000

    b. Inventory—Work-In-Process OH   1,000
          Accumulated Depreciation—Machine   1,000

    c. Depreciation Expense   4,000
          Accumulated Depreciation—Machine   4,000

    d. Inventory—Work-In-Process OH   1,000
          Depreciation Expense   1,000

29. What is the journal entry to record depreciation for a manufacturing company that uses the machine entirely for the production of inventory?

    a. Depreciation Expense   1,000
         Accumulated Depreciation—Machine   1,000

    b. Inventory—Work-In-Process OH   1,000
         Accumulated Depreciation—Machine   1,000

    c. Depreciation Expense   1,000
         Inventory—Work-In-Process OH   1,000

    d. Inventory—Work-In-Process OH   4,000
         Accumulated Depreciation—Machine   4,000

30. How is depreciation recorded for a manufacturer using the machine 70% for the production of inventory?

    a. Inventory—Work-In-Process OH   700
        Depreciation Expense   300
         Accumulated Depreciation—Machine   1,000

    b. Inventory—Work-In-Process OH   1,000
         Accumulated Depreciation—Machine   1,000

    c. Inventory—Work-In-Process OH   3,600
        Depreciation Expense   400
         Inventory—Work-In-Process OH   4,000

    d. Depreciation Expense   1,000
         Accumulated Depreciation—Machine   1,000

Use the following information to answer Questions 31–33: On September 2, 2007, a calendar-year company purchases a new machine (5-year property) for $132,000.

31. What is the maximum tax deduction for the machine in 2007?

   a. $26,400   b. $126,000   c. $125,000   d. $126,400

32. What is the maximum tax deduction for the machine in 2008?

   a. $27,429   b. $2,240   c. $8,640   d. $42,240

33. What is the maximum tax deduction for the machine in 2011 (Year 6)?

   a. $0, because the machine has a 5-year recovery period
   b. $403
   c. $624
   d. $6,451

34. On October 20 of the current year, a company with a December 31 year-end purchases a factory for $150,000, which includes $50,000 for the land. What is first-year depreciation for this asset under MACRS?

   a. $535   b. $53,500   c. $111   d. $2,461

35. Which of the following is *not* subject to annual IRS depreciation limits?

   a. An unmodified company van weighing 5,000 pounds
   b. An unmodified company van weighing 7,500 pounds
   c. A company car used by the company's sales manager
   d. A company car used by the company's president

Use the following information to answer Questions 36–42: A company that uses a calendar year purchases an asset with a historical cost of $250,000, a residual value of $5,000 and an estimated life of 5 years.

36. Under the straight-line method, the depreciation rate is . . .

      a. 40%   b. 20%   c. 10%   d. 5%

37. If the asset is acquired on September 30, 2007, first-year depreciation under the straight-line method is . . .

      a. $50,000   b. $49,000   c. $25,000   d. $12,250

38. If the asset is acquired on January 1, 2007, first-year depreciation under the double-declining balance method is . . .

      a. 40%   b. 20%   c. 25%   d. 5%

39. If the asset is acquired on January 1, 2007, and is depreciated under the double-declining balance method, second-year depreciation is . . .

      a. $100,000   b. $60,000   c. $50,000   d. $25,000

40. If the asset is depreciated under the sum-of- the-years'-digits method, the denominator of the depreciation rate would be . . .

      a. 55   b. 20   c. 15   d. 5

41. If the asset is acquired on January 1, 2007, and is depreciated under the sum-of-the-years'-digits method, first-year depreciation (rounded) would be . . .

      a. $81,667   b. $60,000   c. $49,000   d. $20,417

42. Under any GAAP depreciation method, the maximum depreciation permitted over the asset's life is . . .

      a. $255,000   b. $250,000   c. $245,000   d. $200,000

Use the following information to answer Questions 43–45: A company purchases a machine that has an original cost of $11,500, transportation costs of $500, installation charges of $1,500, an estimated life of 4 years or 20,484 hours, and a residual value of $800. You are depreciating the machine for book purposes.

43. What is the depreciation rate (rounded) under the units of production method?

     a. $0.52 per hour
     b. $0.55 per hour
     c. $0.62 per hour
     d. $0.66 per hour

44. If the machine is acquired on August 1 and is used 2,500 hours during the year, depreciation for the year under the units of production method is . . .

     a. $3,375   b. $3,175   c. $1,550   d. $625

45. Over the first 4 years, the machine is used for 18,000 hours. In Year 5, the machine is used for 3,000 hours. Under the units-of-production method, Year-5 depreciation is . . .

     a. $0   b. $1,540   c. $1,860   d. $2,484

Use the following information to answer Questions 46–50: On April 1, 2007, a company that uses a calendar year purchases equipment with an acquisition cost of $85,000 that it estimates will produce 800,000 units over its 8-year life and have a residual value of $5,000. You are depreciating the asset for book purposes.

46. If the company uses the straight-line method, 2007 depreciation will be . . .

   a. $10,625   b. $10,000   c. $7,969   d. $7,500

47. If the company uses units of production depreciation and the equipment produces 75,000 units in 2007 and 150,000 units in 2008, then at the end of the second year, total accumulated depreciation will be . . .

   a. $80,000   b. $22,500   c. $15,000   d. $7,500

48. If the company uses double-declining balance depreciation, its 2007 depreciation (rounded) will be . . .

   a. $15,938   b. $13,333   c. $10,000   d. $7,500

49. Under double-declining balance depreciation, the equipment's book value (rounded) at the end of 2008 will be . . .

   a. $69,063   b. $67,500   c. $51,797   d. $47,813

50. If the company uses the sum-of-the-years'-digits method, the 2008 depreciation will be (rounded) . . .

   a. $17,778   b. $15,556   c. $16,111   d. $13,333

NOTES

Final Examination Answer Sheet
MASTERING DEPRECIATION

Instructions: Detach this sheet before starting your final examination. Select the letter of the correct answer for each question, then fill in the parallel lines (ǀ ǀ) right beneath that letter. Please use a #2 pencil to make a dark impression. When completed, return to: AIPB Continuing Education, Suite 500, 6001 Montrose Road, Rockville, MD 20852. If you achieve a grade of at least 70, you will receive the Institute's *Certificate of Completion*. Final Examinations are not returned.

For *Certified Bookkeeper* applicants only: If you achieve a grade of at least 70, and become a *Certified Bookkeeper* within three years, you will receive retroactively seven (7) Continuing Professional Education Credits (CPECs) toward the *Certified Bookkeeper* continuing education requirements.

	a	b	c	d			a	b	c	d			a	b	c	d			a	b	c	d
1.	☐	☐	☐	☐	14.	☐	☐	☐	☐	27.	☐	☐	☐	☐	39.	☐	☐	☐	☐
2.	☐	☐	☐	☐	15.	☐	☐	☐	☐	28.	☐	☐	☐	☐	40.	☐	☐	☐	☐
3.	☐	☐	☐	☐	16.	☐	☐	☐	☐	29.	☐	☐	☐	☐	41.	☐	☐	☐	☐
4.	☐	☐	☐	☐	17.	☐	☐	☐	☐	30.	☐	☐	☐	☐	42.	☐	☐	☐	☐
5.	☐	☐	☐	☐	18.	☐	☐	☐	☐	31.	☐	☐	☐	☐	43.	☐	☐	☐	☐
6.	☐	☐	☐	☐	19.	☐	☐	☐	☐	32.	☐	☐	☐	☐	44.	☐	☐	☐	☐
7.	☐	☐	☐	☐	20.	☐	☐	☐	☐	33.	☐	☐	☐	☐	45.	☐	☐	☐	☐
8.	☐	☐	☐	☐	21.	☐	☐	☐	☐	34.	☐	☐	☐	☐	46.	☐	☐	☐	☐
9.	☐	☐	☐	☐	22.	☐	☐	☐	☐	35.	☐	☐	☐	☐	47.	☐	☐	☐	☐
10.	☐	☐	☐	☐	23.	☐	☐	☐	☐	36.	☐	☐	☐	☐	48.	☐	☐	☐	☐
11.	☐	☐	☐	☐	24.	☐	☐	☐	☐	37.	☐	☐	☐	☐	49.	☐	☐	☐	☐
12.	☐	☐	☐	☐	25.	☐	☐	☐	☐	38.	☐	☐	☐	☐	50.	☐	☐	☐	☐
13.	☐	☐	☐	☐	26.	☐	☐	☐	☐										

_____   _____ / ____ / ____
Name (Please print clearly)   Title   Date

_____
Company   Street Address

_____
City   State   Zip

For *Certified Bookkeeper* applicants only: #_____
                    Membership or Certification (nonmember) ID Number

Course Evaluation for
MASTERING DEPRECIATION

Please complete and return (even if you do not take the Final Examination) to: AIPB Continuing Education, Suite 500, 6001 Montrose Road, Rockville, MD 20852. **PLEASE PRINT CLEARLY.**

Circle one

1. Did you find the instructions clear?   Yes   No

Comments: _____

_____

2. Did you find the course practical?   Yes   No

Comments_____

_____

3. Is this course what you expected?   Yes   No

Comments_____

_____

4. Would you recommend this course to other accounting professionals?   Yes   No

Comments: _____

_____

5. What did you like most about *Mastering Depreciation*? _____

_____

6. What would have made the course even more helpful? _____

_____

7. May we use your comments and name in advertising for the course?   Yes   No

8. Would you be interested in other courses?   Yes   No

Please indicate what subject areas would be of greatest interest to you: _____

1. _____   3. _____

2. _____   4. _____

Name (optional)   Title   Date

                                  /   /

Company   Street Address

City   State   Zip   Phone Number

NOTES

NOTES